THE ENTERTAINERS
GEORGE FORMBY

The Entertainers
Edited by Philip Oakes

GEORGE FORMBY

John Fisher

Woburn-Futura

For Mike Parkinson

First published in Great Britain in 1975 by Woburn-Futura
110 Warner Road, London S.E.5

Copyright © John Fisher 1975

ISBN 0 7130 0139 9

Printed in Great Britain by Butler & Tanner Ltd, Frome and London

Designed by Gilvrie Misstear

Acknowledgements

I am grateful to many people who in giving freely of their memories and impressions have helped make the picture of George Formby in these pages as complete as possible. In alphabetical order they are: Chesney Allen, Arthur Askey, Sir Michael Balcon, Lady Isobel Barnett, George Bartram, Sir John Betjeman, Peter Brough, Phyllis Calvert, Bill Cotton, Monja Danischewsky, Les Dawson, Basil Dean, Benson Dulay, Peter Dulay, Richard Evans, Gracie Fields, Hughie Green, Irene Handl, Kathleen Harrison, Tony Hawes, Robert Holmes, Roy Hudd, Mr and Mrs Nat Jackley, John Jackson, Alan Kennaugh, Pat Kirkwood, Sir Emile Littler, A. L. Lloyd, William Logan, Eve Lucas, Garry Marsh, Albert Modley, Professor Wilfrid Mellers, John Kennedy Melling, George Melly, Alan Randall, Ted Ray, Bettina Richman (Mrs John Jackson), Don Ross, Ray Seaton, Harry Secombe, Alastair Sim, Terry-Thomas, Barry Took, Tommy Trinder, and Max Wall. I should also like to record my gratitude for the enthusiasm received during the early stages of the project from Colin Webb; the help of Maggie Chapman, Vivien Green, Gilvrie Misstear, and Lynette Trotter; the unflagging support of Richard Simon; as well as the faith and encouragement of Philip Oakes.   J.F.

Picture Credits

British Film Institute 32–33, 40–41, 54–55, 64–65
John Fisher 39, 61, 84–85
Ronald Grant 7, 11, 50–51, 52, 54–55, 57, 58–59
Keystone Press Agency 80
Bill Logan, George Formby Society 18, 26–27, 35, 41, 43, 45, 67, 70–71, 75
Mander-Mitchenson Collection 21
Popperfoto 12–13, 14, 22, 42, 48, 63, 72–73, 82, 84–85, 86, 88–89, 92
Radio Times Hulton Picture Library 46, 77

Picture research by Lynette Trotter

The music of time

He was in retrospect my introduction to nostalgia, the first intimation that access is possible to the pleasures of an age denied us by time, that I had not completely missed out by being born too late. In the dust-free, Ronuk-scented shrine of the suburban front room to which entry was allowed only on Sunday afternoons I was initiated into the Formby cult. It was the Festival of Britain era and when the radio palled, expecially in the lulls between those motley half-hours which now stand as milestones in the history of radio comedy – *Take It From Here, Educating Archie, Ray's a Laugh, The Goon Show* – entertainment was provided by those sounds which unwound from an upright gramophone, coffined in sturdy veneer. Among the dusty 78's were records as diverse as those of Rawicz and Landauer and the Inkspots, of Bing Crosby and anonymous brass bands, and, a distinct novelty, a disc of radio favourites, Bebe Daniels and Ben Lyon, warbling their way through "Elmer's Tune". But – except for the latter – I had little time for these, tolerated them for my parents' sake. Only the records of George Formby, so attractive to a child of seven with his jaunty tunes and shy, sly chuckle, instilled a decided craving to sample his complete repertoire, however long it might take. More than any entertainer, Formby then held the key to a Utopia in reverse.

Inappropriately, the first song I recall him singing was one of the few he recorded that had not been specially composed for him; but with its chirpy moderato and sexy suggestiveness, it is hard to believe that "Hi-Tiddly-Hi-Ti Island" had been written as early as 1922, before Formby ever fondled a uke. Its South Sea Island motif provided the perfect setting for listening to his distinctive ukulele twang for the first time. The name, "ukulele", in fact derives from the comparison drawn by the King of Hawaii between the nimble fingerwork needed to play the small, four-stringed, treble guitar, introduced to his island by Portuguese traders around 1870, and the dancing of a flea. The Hawaian for "flea" is *uku*, for "to dance" *lele*. From these exotic origins the instrument became streamlined around 1917 by

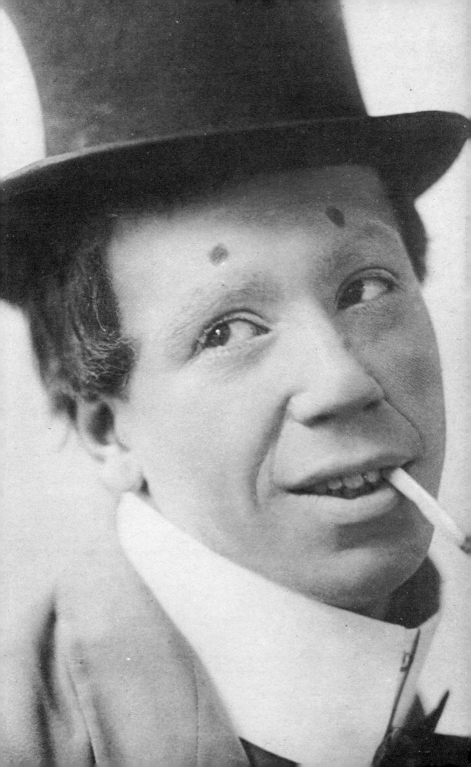

American musical instrument manufacturers Alvin and Mal Keech into the hybrid banjulele. Their pamphlet tutor declared that there was now "no instrument so suitable on the river or picnics, at garden parties, or in the quiet of the home". In time the comedian with the most homely rapport would become wedded to the most compatible of instruments.

On record, however, Formby had far more to offer than a skilled banjulele technique. On looking back one realises that part of his success was due to an instinctive ability to bridge the chasm that divides the artist and his public in the mechanised medium. Apart from his obvious physical presence, there was little of his appeal that he was unable to maintain in the disembodiment of his voice. In recording he was one of the few authentic music-hall names who never lost his contact with the unseen audience. His buoyant, flat-capped, Lancashire tones somehow conveyed the full glow of the smile that spread across his face like a rosy sunrise over the factory skyline. To respond to his sunbeam quality on a stage was to feel that you knew him, so he was half-way across your threshold before you even purchased the record. But there was a two-way traffic at work here. On stage his presence confirmed what his success in front parlours throughout the nation had hinted, and his elevation to star-status of one of the most "do-it-yourself" of musical instruments had further underlined, namely that if throughout his career he projected one clearly defined persona, it was that of the enthusiastically talented amateur singing, joking, strumming for the sheer kick he got out of it. Towards the end of his life, he himself would admit: "I wasn't very good, but I had something the public seemed to want." Luckily he never questioned what that something might be. As a result, his share of that magic which so few performers possess, the magic which can transcend originality, charm, likeability, technique, even talent, escaped erosion; his sense of wonder that he should have arrived on a stage at all remained that of a five-year-old. And yet the further the rare quality, one hostile to rational analysis, is stressed, so the question is begged more urgently just how consciously clever an artist Formby was, how much that radiant display of selfhood concealed a precise technique.

The secret of Formby's art rested in its apparent artlessness. He must have known that any attempt at a Bob Hope slickness in his delivery of a line would have been disastrous; certainly nature saw that the sheer repetition of his well-worn gags brought them no closer to the polished treatment of his contemporaries. Despite the contrary evidence of his flustered hen walk, he was nothing if not surefooted in the way he conducted his act through from start to finish with immaculate ease. But if this was skilled technique, the secret was not to make a fuss about it. In this way he retained his innocence, all the while shrewdly deleting anything in the end product that might suggest artful contrivance. Moreover, at the core of his technique was a gyroscopic ability for maintaining an instinctive equilibrium at the conclusion of the most complicated routines. Phyllis Calvert recalls how during the filming of *Let George Do It*, in a scene where he has to pass from one to another of five separate doors in turn, only to find his way blocked by the enemy at each, he would, without rehearsal, unerringly finish the song he was singing all this time at the precise moment he arrived at the final door. The same innate timing graced another scene where he gets out of bed singing, washes, shaves, gets dressed, only to hit the final note of the song as he fastens the last button of his coat. It is evident in even the slightest gesture. Bashfully taken aback at his first meeting with Miss Calvert, in a moment reminiscent of the befuddled finesse of W. C. Fields with hat and cane, he throws up one arm for no other reason than that of dismayed embarrassment and then, as a split-second afterthought, intuitively uses that hand to doff his hat while it chances to be hovering in the area. He is drawn to do so subconsciously as if to maintain comic balance. If it had been rehearsed it would have looked contrived. Without question the ease and inevitability with which he handled such incidents are part of an expertise which can be traced back to the sturdy music-hall background into which he was born, Formby as a comedian holding the rare distinction of becoming the even more famous son of a famous comedian father.

From Wigan and proud of it...

George Formby Senior, or "The Wigan Nightingale" as his billing insisted, while never ceasing to be a gentle comedian, epitomised more vividly than any performer before or since the hard fact that all great North Country humour is born out of misery and deprivation, the sheer grimness of the environment which it sets out to alleviate. The pivot of his act was a real-life bronchial condition. As well as enhancing his accent, evocative of industrial smoke and the rasp of coal dust, it was responsible for a persistent hacking cough which provided plaintive comic punctuation to the portrayal of his character John Willie, the archetypal gormless Lancashire lad. "Coughin' better tonight, coughin' summat champion," he would confide to the musical director; "Come on – I'll cough you for a shilling," he would challenge the orchestra; "Bronchitis – I'm a bit tight tonight – on chest. I could do with a strengthening bottle," he would admit prior to his final curtain. Everything about his appearance, from clogs which had found their way onto the wrong feet, through baggy, concertina-crumpled trousers, to gloves with more holes than fingers and hunched shoulders emphasising the tight fit of his jacket, contributed to his sad Chaplinesque air in a pre-Chaplin era. In contrast, his songs were afizz with gaiety and champagne, their titles suggesting one never-ending spree: "I'm Such a Hit with the Girls", "Looking for Mugs in the Strand", "Since I Parted My Hair in the Middle", "One of the Boys". One of his most celebrated numbers had him "Playing the game in the West", a self-appointed dare-devil or young dog so overwhelmed at being set loose in the big bad city where money could be splashed around like water and girls grew on trees, that he was determined not to return home till a quarter to ten on this, his one big night out. But however much his socialite *manqué* failed to justify itself amongst what he considered superior company, however much audiences laughed at his shyness and failed aspirations, they always laughed more at the cough that cut him down to size, even though cold statistics would have reminded them that the mortality rate from bronchitis in that surprisingly exposed north west corner of

George's father complete with cut-down bowler and pre-Chaplin cane

the country was, still is, 20 per cent above the national average. But they *could* laugh because no one ever thought there might be any truth in the specific case-history which Formby transmuted into comic gold.

The cough, at first painful, eventually proved fatal on 8th February 1921, when the strain tore a number of blood vessels in his larynx and a haemorrhage ensued. He was in his early forties and had long been aware of the severity of his condition, that the laughter he achieved taunted death itself. Max Wall, who worked with him on one of his last bills, remembers vividly the oxygen tent always in readiness at the side of the stage. The pull of the boards, however, and a natural desire to make as ample future provision for his family as possible in the years dwindling away fast both triumphed over common sense, annulling any chance of recuperation in preference to his nightly show of masochistic bravado. He will be remembered, however, as more than one of the most tragic figures to emerge from a notoriously precarious profession. The most telling measure of his

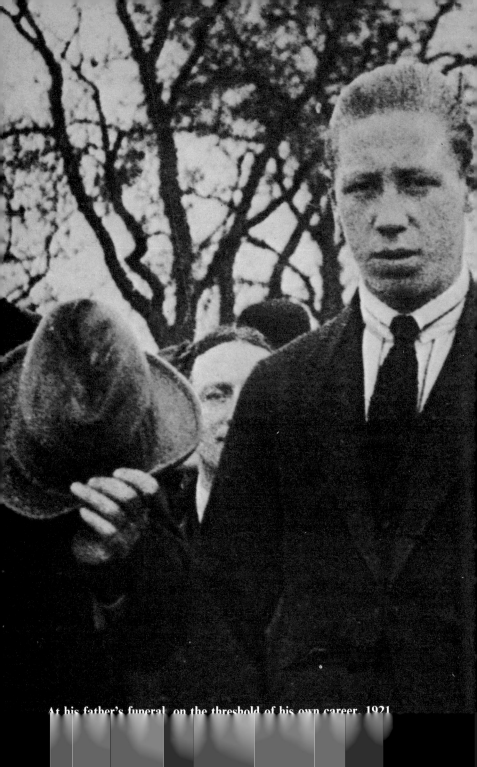

At his father's funeral, on the threshold of his own career, 1921

talent and status is that Marie Lloyd, the undisputed Queen of the Halls, would herself deign to watch only two of her contemporaries; one was Dan Leno, the other George Formby Senior.

He bequeathed an inventory of gambits and catchphrases which would enter music-hall lore. The inconsequential "Oh, a big blood orange will do!" used by many subsequent comics, was the original suggestion of his wife Eliza in their frustration to finish a line in a song, "If you can't get a nice little girl ..." He was the first to make real comic play out of the delayed entrance: his number would go up in the frame at the side of the stage, the orchestra would start, then stop, the expectant silence that ensued only broken by his lugubrious quaver, "I'm ready." The band would play again and he was on. But this way the audience was laughing before he ever appeared. Above everything else, however, it was George Formby's fertile imagination that invented Wigan Pier, or at least so christened the small landing stage on the branch of the recently opened (1894) Manchester Ship Canal that connected Wigan with Warrington:

"Aw right, aw right ... it's aw right you lot laughin'. It's very nice is Wigan Pier. Ah've been there many times in my bathing costume and dived off the highboard int' water. Next time you go on holiday to Wigan, make sure you visit t' pier...." Comedians still make jokes about that small map speck of a landing stage. His son was born in the town and when questioned about his origins never ceased to take pride in the fact, to perpetuate the memory of his father's fictional monument: "Ah'm just an ordinary Lancashire lad. Ah suppose you'd call me a pup of Wigan Pier." He knew that for all the cotton, coal and calico, he would never forgo the distinction, his by inheritance, of being the most famous Northern product to embark upon a useful life from that quay.

Horses and courses

Unlike his father, George Formby was not a product of cobbled-street poverty and privation. George Senior, born illegitimate, and a singing beggar by apprenticeship, was secure enough now in his profession to command a weekly income of around £300 throughout his son's infancy. The circumstances surrounding the latter's birth, however, contain their own grim irony. He was born blind in Wigan on 26th May 1904, and would not be able to see until some weeks later when a coughing fit – luckily free from bronchial associations – removed the obstructive caul while he was crossing the River Mersey as a babe in his mother's arms. There is no trace of any other hardship in George's early life. Music-hall legend Gertie Gitana recalled for her husband, impresario Don Ross, a visit paid her by George and his mother when she was playing the Argyle, Birkenhead. His appearance would have done credit to Little Lord Fauntleroy; his fascination in his new white celluloid collar so great that he could not stop looking in the mirror and rubbing it with his coat sleeve: "Eee, mother, don't it shine?"

From the first, father had been adamant that son was not destined for the boards. Late in life that son remarked, "I never saw Dad on the stage. He wouldn't let me. He used to say, 'One fool in the family's enough.'" Formby could remember from his earliest years his father coming home tired, worn and ill, and did not at first quarrel with the healthy outdoor life his parents planned for him as an alternative. At the age of seven he was despatched to a riding stable for training as an apprentice jockey, his parents able in time to go to the expense of buying him several mounts of his own. His family associations with the turf on his mother's side were strong. His grandfather, born at Newmarket, had worked as a professional jockey, while even more remarkably two of his mother's uncles had been respectively head postillion to King Umberto of Italy and a groom at Buckingham Palace in Victoria's reign. Within this context the fact that Formby became the youngest jockey to compete professionally when at ten years old – weighing no more than three stone thirteen pounds – he 15 entered a race under Lord Derby's colours, becomes no more surprising than that he should eventually break theatre records in his father's footsteps. That he did one day tread the boards was a culmination of circumstances that included his own eventual overweight, his father's death, and the subsequent plagiarism of his father's manner and material by an inferior Tyneside comic, Tommy Dixon, spotted by George through chance at the Victoria Palace on a rare visit to London with his mother to recover from the shock of bereavement. He never went back to the stables, his promise never to go on the stage now outweighed by the determination with which he decided that if anyone had a right to a father's creation, it was his son. He did maintain one scruple, however, namely that he would not assume the name of Formby until he was top of the bill in his own right. In actual fact the family name was Booth; George's father had seen the name "Formby" on a coal-wagon in the sidings at Wigan station and used it as a stage name out of sheer whim. George, however, would not even trade on 'Booth' and adopted instead his mother's maiden name.

It was as George Hoy that he made his first professional appearance in April 1921 as part of a cine-variety bill at the Hippodrome, Earlestown, later dismissed by the entertainer as "a little tin hut near Newton-le-Willows". In that first act all he could offer was a poor imitation of the father he had never seen perform. The impersonation was force-fed on a striking visual similarity which included the two red spots branded by make-up on his forehead, a practical, if surprising, substitute for eyes rendered invisible in the glare of the footlights – a likeness not too difficult for his mother, anxious no doubt to resurrect her husband as much as to advance her son in an alien profession, to effect – and the diligent study of his father's scratchy recordings. There was one omission – the cough, at last, with his father's fate well known, too painful for comedy. For three years Formby was initiated into the hard grind and shabby insecurity of touring variety, until in August 1924 he was rewarded with a West End booking at the Alhambra, the most prestigious variety theatre in the country. Here was the burlesque of the would-be gay blade in the manner of his father singing appropriately "I'm a Jockey"; but also, as if to emphasise he had constructive ideas of his own, a skit on an anarchist complete with plum-pudding bomb, sinister sweeping cloak, and slouch hat. From around this time dates another

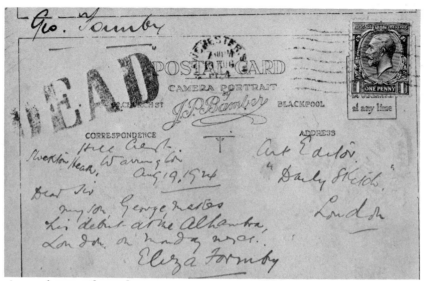

An anxious mother volunteers as press agent, 1924

sketch set in an auctioneer's: George discovers he has bought six
picture postcards for sixpence: "Eeee – I've been done – they've got
no stamps." Also a burlesque of another of nature's losers, a man
with one leg in plaster who has to strike a compromise of balance
as he fends off with his two sticks the dog pestering it.

By the time he reached the Alhambra he *was* using his father's
stage name. George had been booked as the first act, the warm-up
spot. And yet, as if to drive home to him that there was no disgrace
attached to answering to the name of Formby, the musical director,
George Saker, whose usual practice was not to appear until later in
the programme when the audience had settled in, pre-empted the
makeshift presence of his deputy and strode down the aisle with all
his usual ceremony immediately prior to the first act, out of tribute
to father by way of not a little encouragement to his son. It was at
the Alhambra that he added his catchphrase, always delivered with
that warm throaty chuckle, which was in ironic contrast with his
father's hacking cough: "It's turned out nice again, hasn't it." The
phrase was indicative. For three years he had had to live down the
kind of criticism that insisted he was exceedingly pale fire beside his
father. On his first appearance at the Argyle, Birkenhead, a stage his
father had dominated often, pennies had been tossed at his feet and
he had been forced to leave the stage. But two events would in turn 17

The 'camera portrait'
his mother sent plus
an earlier bill

MORECAMBE
TOWER

THEATRE, BALLROOM & GARDENS.
General Manager H. R. V. ADDENBROOKE

PREMIER PLACE OF ENTERTAINMENT IN MORECAMBE

Week
Commencing MONDAY, SEPT. 10th, 1923

TWICE DAILY at 2 and 7 p.m.

FIRST VISIT TO MORECAMBE OF

DOROT

WOO

The famous Violinist and Composer of "Roses of Picardy"

At the Piano, LIL

WM ULLERING

THE ACT BEAUTIFUL

Featuring "LILLIEU" a pure White Arabian Mare, and English Setter Dogs, in an Artistic Posing Novelty

TOM FAGAN | HALMA
AND HIS PACK | THE CRAZY DANCING JUGGLER

KEITH and JOAN DINGLEY
PRESENTING A NOVELTY DANCING SCENA

Morecambe's Largest and Finest Ballroom Floor   Laid on 3,000 Springs.

DANCING

(Every Afternoon and Evening) IN THE TUDOR BALLROOM (Latest Carnival Novelties)
THE SCARLET JAZZ ORCHESTRA.
THE MYSTIC CARNIVAL LANTERN, designed by H R V Addenbrooke (Patent applied for).

SATURDAY NIGHT, 15th SEPTEMBER.

FANCY DRESS CARNIVAL : 2 BANDS

BERT NEILSON
THE ROYAL NON-STOP DANCER

MAFAZIANG MANCHU TROUPE
OF CHINESE WONDERS

GEORGE | FRED
FORMBY | HUTCHINGS
JUNR. | THE LADY OF LAUGHS
CHIP OFF THE OLD BLOCK

GRAND CONCERTS EACH SUNDAY.   See Bills.

MATINEES VARIETY AND DANCING DAILY at 2 p.m.

PRICES (INCLUDING TAX)

Upper Circle or Promenade	PIT	PIT STALLS	DRESS CIRCLE	ORCH STALLS
1/-	1/3	2/-	2/4	3/-
CHILD 6d.	CHILD 9d.	CHILD 1/-	CHILD 1/2	CHILD 1/6

Reserved Seats, Dress Circle 2/10, Orchestra Stalls 3/6.   Box Office Now Open. Tel. 116
Children not admitted to Evening Performances unless accompanied by a Guardian. The Management reserve the right to refuse Admission, to change the entertainment or portions thereof and may not entitle the person so applying to take out of the Tower and dancing by virtue of such payment, not to guarantee the appearance of any Artiste whose name is included in the advertisement

SPECIAL LATE TRAIN SERVICE
To Leicester (Central) 10-15 p.m. and 10-45 p.m. Daily.   Also 11 p.m. Wednesdays and Saturdays.
To Lancaster (Midland) 9-40 p.m., 10-00 p.m. and 10-40 p.m.
To Carnforth, Kendal and Various Lines, 10-40 p.m.
To Leicester (Midland), Halton, Caton, Hornby, Wennington, 9-45 p.m. Daily. Also 10-40 p.m.

GILLOW, PRINTER.

set him securely on the path whereby he would establish a claim even to the affections of the most loyal followers of George Formby Senior.

"For a lark", as he later admitted, he bought for fifty shillings a banjulele off a colleague with whom he happened to be sharing a dressing room. A noisome habit of strumming aimlessly in digs and back stage on tour prompted a friendly taunt from a pair of singers, one-time friends of his father, the outcome of which was a challenge to play it on stage. The tune he fell back upon to make theatrical history was "Going back to Tennessee". That night at the Alhambra Theatre, Barnsley, Formby first experienced the exhilaration of an audience clamouring for more. Another version of the story has the manager of the theatre pulling the carpet from beneath Formby's feet towards the end of the Barnsley week by deploying his younger brother, Frank Formby, to confront him on stage with the official instruction: "The management have told me you've got to play this." Anyhow, he now had the gimmick that would draw what talent he possessed to the attention of the right people. But those four strings did more than help to cut his ties with his father's well-worn routine. They also played their part in serenading the first person perceptive enough to see that George had a quality beyond talent.

Formby met his wife Beryl, one half of the sister team "The Two Violets", a clog-dancing speciality, when playing in revue at Castleford in 1923. Her first impression of his act was straight to the point: "If I'd had a bag of rotten tomatoes with me I'd have thrown them at him." Neither this nor the impetuous nature of his proposals, however, prevented their eventual marriage in September the following year. It was, in fact, under Beryl's influence that he adopted the Formby name as a more commercial proposition for theatre managements, was eventually swayed to make the ukulele the focal point of his routine, and first gave proper attention to stage presentation. Above all, it was she who saw the magic and warmth crystallised in his shy awkward smile. She herself had been a champion clog dancer. It would not be long before she would qualify as a champion business enterpreneuse. It is doubtful if, but for her, he would have made it so big. Indeed, it was her influence, and not his, that in 1925 secured the first booking for the new edition of George Formby, a six months' contract at the fabulous fee of £15 a week, again with irony at the Empire, Newcastle, where his father had fallen fatally ill. 19

As the chief catalyst in his career, Beryl smartened him up as she smoothed him down. Even today a mistaken cloth-cap image of him as a north-country comedian persists; but George after Beryl's treatment was nothing if not immaculately turned out, from the dark Brylcreem-slick hair with its disciplinary parting and the shellac sheen of one of his own gramophone records, to the resplendent dinner jacket worn at all times on stage during his standard act. When in the song "It's in the Air" he sang of feeling "so smart and debonair", his words rang truer than the memory of him as a quintessential Northern comedian today allows. Although his appeal was straight to the ordinary man, he was in stage appearance classless. In one respect he was even ahead of his time. Until Jack Benny and Danny Kaye invaded the Palladium in the late 'forties it was hard to name a top British stand-up comedian who did not possess his identifying headpiece, whether Flanagan with battered boater, Askey with pilot's cap, Jimmy James his alcohol-conscious derby, Eddie Gray that soaring topper, Miller, Trinder, Ray, Handley with their assorted trilbies – the hat of the 'thirties – at assorted angles, not to mention the cloth caps. The hat proved you were a comedian; was an extension of your total expression. In a double act it often established the pecking order. More than one comic has been heard to explain to a straight man bent on upstaging: "I'm wearing the hat, I get the laughs." Formby, no doubt at his wife's insistence, shunned all styles, above all the cut-down bowler of his father. Under Beryl's Svengali-like guidance the air of good-natured, gormless naivety that had informed his father's characterisation was burnished free of any traces of melancholy and mock despair. His son developed a lighter, fresher approach, typified in his films not so much by the resilience with which he met the blows dealt out by fate but by the smile of everlasting wonder that appeared as he met them.

His stage act became utterly predictable, varying little from that featured Newcastle appearance until his premature death, an unpretentious mixture of the broad catchy songs for which single-handed he would carve a niche in British folk-lore, and tired, haggard, out-of-date jokes from which he would squeeze, like Mr Wu his washing, that one last drop of moisture. He made a speciality of parrot gags, like "Knock Knock", one of the silly joke crazes of the day, in the way that Freddie Davies today chronicles the zanier activities of the budgerigar species. There was the one about an entertainer

who tells an impresario that he impersonates a parrot, and when told that bird-impersonators are two-a-penny says "Pity", turns and flies out of the window. On paper they appear the type of jokes with which a son would be hard pressed to amuse a more-than-doting mother, and yet the combination of a reassuring familiarity and his own unstinted enjoyment in putting them across, as if he had only just heard them himself, still made for laughter. His delivery had the ring of conversational chat rather than of slick patter, echoing the rhythms of the way people, more so in the North, pass the time of day with each other, even if when they do speak they say the same things over and over again. This made him a natural for confiding domestic trivia to an audience, and there is evidence to show that had he completely dropped the gags from his chat he would have won over even more fans. Terry-Thomas recalls how puzzled he was when in the revue *Fun and the Fair*, the occasion of Formby's last Palladium appearance in October 1953, he, not George, was given the next-to-finale closing spot, while Formby's own act closed the first half. All the evidence salary and publicity-wise indicated that George was undisputed top-of-the-bill. After Thomas himself had gone less than well on opening night he asked producer Charles Henry why he didn't put George in the star spot at the end, which, like the No. 1 dressing room, was his by right: "What, with all those fucking stories!" came the reply. But it didn't matter—as long as he still had two things: a personality capable of melting an audience in the crucible of his hand and what he described with characteristic simplicity as "me daft little songs".

Composition for 'uke' and cigarette holder?: George with Terry-Thomas at the Palladium, 1953

Songs for a comic post-card

At the peak of his career Formby churned out records at the rate of one a month, first mainly for Decca and then for EMI on the Regal Zonophone label. He recorded no fewer than 189 songs, and when the EMI contract expired in 1946, people supposed that the supply had run dry, a thought confirmed when Decca invited him back to re-record his most famous numbers in 1950. And yet after his death over two hundred unrecorded songs were unearthed. For evidence of his popularity in the fashionable recording medium one has to look no further than the little girl who when introduced to Formby replied, "That's not George Formby – George Formby is a record." It was another way of saying that the combination of voice and banjulele was the man, the most distinctly identifiable sound the British music-hall tradition ever produced.

His cracked tones had all the subtlety of a factory whistle, yet, nothing if not jaunty and enthusiastic, they were the perfect complement to his strum-machine. Even Kenneth Tynan, in a harsh review of *Zip Goes a Million* as late as 1951, had to concede that his piercing, sunny little voice was "one of the pleasantest in London". It was also as unmistakably Lancashire as the clumping of the mill-girls' clogs down the stone street, the clanking of the machines they worked. Musically it had a neglible quality, but what it lacked in vocal range was made up for in his faultless pointing of the lyrics, the instinctive jogging of his swivel-neck to right or left and the suggestive wink emphasising those crucial moments of double entendre with the casual precision of a metronome. Given the basic innocence he portrayed, it is a valid question to ask whether he fully understood the double meanings rife in his lyrics. One has only to listen carefully for that carefully placed "H":

> Now in a young lady's bedroom I went quite by mistake,
> My intentions were honest you see,

the instinctive chuckle sustained in spirit through the subsequent lines:

23

But she shouted with laughter – *he-he* –
I know what you're after,
Me Auntie Maggie's remedy

to realise that he was determined one would not miss even the most obvious point.

Without the bounce, snap and bite of his ukulele technique, the songs themselves were not musically inspiring, the majority formulaic permutations of a handful of basic tunes. This sense of repetition, as with his patter, stands as its own metaphor for the lifeless drudgery lived by the bulk of his audience, like Blackpool – his perfect milieu – an extension of the working-class treadmill, but gift-wrapped. Formby possessed a select reserve of "cheering up songs" – titles like, "Count Your Blessings and Smile" and "Swinging Along Singing a Song" – but that essential "this'll make you whistle" quality was present in everything he sang, a quality reinforced by the performer's conviction that soon you would be doing just that, as well as by his triumphant arm's-length flourish of the uke out of sheer joy at the end of each number.

For the most part his vocal repertoire was the musical counterpart of a spinning wire rack of seaside comic postcards in the manner of Donald McGill. The parallel is unmistakable, the common ground that world of appalling well-upholstered wives, their weedy, henpecked husbands, and nudists either brazen or bashful but never in between, of faulty plumbing, multiple births and satin bloomers waving defiantly in the breeze. It was a world where prunes and sennapods comprised the staple diet, the gout was the greatest calamity that could befall Man, and passing eels were always ready for the grasping by prim females just below sea level. McGill himself had doubtless been influenced by the bawdry of the music hall; when he married in 1900 it was in fact to the daughter of a music-hall proprietor. With Formby things came full circle. It is somewhat prophetic that the first postcard McGill drew, in 1904, was of a man up to his waist in the broken ice of a pond, with the caption "Hope you'll be out soon", an attempt to cheer up a nephew in hospital. The song which Formby himself regarded as his first big hit, from his first film *Boots! Boots!*, carried the title, "Sitting on the Ice in the Ice Rink". But the similarity extended beyond the subject matter to its treatment. The persistent rhythms which underline his lyrics exactly parallel the crude, monotonous, yet enlivening stretches of happy colour in the graphic form, the blatant "poetic" licence which often distinguishes the rhyming and word-order of the songs evocative of the blunt forceful quality of the line drawing. Where, however, McGill and his fellow draughtsmen fell short of Formby was in their basic attitude to the world of the people for which they drew, one hidebound by the idea that the more tedious a man's working day, the less exciting his leisure hours, that the greatest adventure that could befall the working class after marriage was its annual visit to the seaside (a truth that persists into the 'seventies if you equate package-tour Majorca with Blackpool). The cards became stereotyped and ultimately boring for the simple reason that however outrageous their perspective, however escapist their function, they were essentially commenting upon a society drab and boring already, the world of the people who bought them. Formby, or at least his writers, saw the dangers of the comment which fails to offer alternatives and injected a strong strain of adventure into their own imagery.

As Orwell pointed out in his classic study of the McGill genre, the seaside postcard was a virtual no-man's land for the foreigner, unless one included the Scotsman with his mini-skirt kilt and scrawny knees. Along the wider horizons which Formby's repertoire embraced paraded a gallery of world-wide exotics who included Frigid Air Fanny from the Argentine who came into England on a cattle boat:

> Don't tell her she's frozen mutton, for if you do,
> Soon you'll get the frozen mitt, and the cold shoulder too'

Madam Moscovitch, the Moscow witch, who for a "bob-ski" will read your palm, but annoyingly only in her native tongue; and yet

> If you pay a quid then she
> Will unfold her mystery
> And you'll see much more
> Than you did before
> Of the Russian Gipsy Queen

and the Indian "Hindoo-Howdoo-Hoodoo-Yoodoo-Man", who spends all day smoking "opium and bits of rope and fag ends besides" and, for all his ninety-nine years:

ALKING to the MOO
ABOUT YOU
Words & Music by Dorothy Day
Sung by George Formby in the Columbia Film
HILDA BAYLEY
JOSS AMBLER
JIMMY CLITHEROE
MY LITTLE WOODEN
TOOL SHED IN THE GARDEN
WRITTEN BY
TED STEELS
GEO. A. STEVENS
AND
CHARLES WILMOTT
Composed & Sung by
6D NET.
Copyright 1939 by Francis, Day & Hun
London: FRANCIS, DAY & HUNTER, Ltd
138-140, Charing Cross Road, W.C.2.

A princess gave him pearls and said "for all your love I
  yearn",
But jewels could not compare with what he went and gave her
  in return.

There was "Hill Billy Willie from the Cowheel Range", tying a
feather duster to his bronco's tail to swish away the flies, as well as
"Don Pedro, the great bullfighting hero, the Lancashire Toreador",
both of whom turned out to be none other than George himself:

They cheer me,
And when the bull gets near me,
To show how far a brave man can go,
With the bull I dance the tango.

Such escapades spotlighted George as the true spirit of adventure
in contrast with the two-dimensional inhabitants of the postcard
world, restricted for their kicks to sex and seaside, alcohol and the
great outdoors. For all he would knock his own prowess:

I'm not a super sort of man,
There isn't much that I can do but sing

he still had to admit

Yet if you watch me at a fight,
I could knock Joe Louis out the ring.

In "The Best of Schemes" he is again "a rascal for sport", dauntlessly
accepting a hundred-pound bet that he can swim the Channel. After
swimming for fourteen hours "with the sea like a lake"

I reached the other side and said, "The money I'll take",
And then I found I'd swum the Serpentine by mistake.

Another good scheme had gone wrong. The intrepid George was
never happier though than when he was "Riding in the T.T.
Races":

Hear the people cheer me when they see me steering backwards,
Down the hill I go at break-neck speed.
See me coming down the street,
With the women posed on the pillion seat,
Oh come along and see me
Riding in the T.T. Races.

Formby knew that however much it might be outside the actual experience of his basic audience, alongside Royalty nothing captured the imagination of those masses more keenly than the world of professional sport.

The conservatively jagged rhythms of Formby's most typical numbers, anchored in a grass-roots ragtime as they were, even went their own adventurous way to celebrate, albeit by parody, while still remaining wholesome Formby material, what were in the 'thirties regarded as more sophisticated, imported musical trends. On the other hand, in no way could the distinctive draughtsmanship of McGill accommodate the equally stylised, but more streamlined graphic styles which in 'thirties America daily immortalised the adventures of heroes like Superman, Flash Gordon, Dick Tracy and Batman, and would come to revolutionise popular art in this country, rescuing it from the rut typified by the earlier *Comic Cuts* tradition. Pure jazz as such was something to be laughed at, as proved by "John Willie's Jazz Band", simultaneously a resuscitation of his father's famous character and a burlesque of an American syncopation specialist. This outfit, however, had not been recruited from Dixieland but amongst the coal-black pitshafts and tripe plantations "down in Wiganland". With that parochial surrealism which Ken Dodd would fully exploit a generation later, their combined musical talents had a habit of turning black puddings white with fear. Inevitably they came to play on Wigan Pier itself, whereupon everyone in earshot proceeded to fill their ears with the mythical sand. In a similar vein were "The Lancashire Hot Pot Swingers" who "blast and blow and blow and blast" with such élan that another swing would set them in orbit around the earth, and that in spite of a cornet player who plays his instrument through his nose and a crooner who has swallowed his false teeth. One of the earliest songs he recorded – so early that the only credit Formby received on the label was that of anonymous "Vocal Refrain" to Jack Hylton and his Band – poked fun at the craze of contemporary (1932) vocalists for attaching the meaningless "Do-de-o-do" to everything they sang. Formby enthusiastically conveys the shrewd idea of latching onto a good thing, though characteristically his own conception of the refrain is punningly restricted to thoughts of money, home cooking, tonic sol-fa, and female rabbits, never the sheer fun of carefree musical improvisation.

Whatever scope Formby's vocal repertoire offered for the variety, adventure and novelty refused to its colourful cardboard counterpart, it *was* in depicting the actual world of the basic *seaside* comic postcard that he was most at home, in the way that if one town qualified as his spiritual home it was Blackpool where in the 'thirties, 'forties and into the 'fifties, summer after summer, the town would never be completely itself without Formby at the top of one bill. Many of his songs boasted a seaside motif, songs like "Sitting on the Sands all Night", "Blackpool Prom" and most outrageous:

> With my little stick of Blackpool rock
> Along the Promenade I stroll;
> In my pocket it got stuck I could tell,
> 'Cos when I pulled it out I pulled my shirt up as well.
> Everyday, wherever I stray, the kids all round me flock;
> A girl while bathing clung to me – my wits had I to use –
> She cried I'm drowning and to save me you won't refuse;
> I said well if you're drowning I don't want to lose
> My little stick of Blackpool Rock.

but it is hard to imagine any of them with their breezy rollicking tunes being written without the people who stroll along that most flaunting, most bracing of promenades in mind. In the same way it is difficult to imagine that round beamish face with its mascot horseshoe grin not being custom-built for insertion in those loud lifesize cutouts which to a beach photographer's delight transform the dullest of old maids into a Miss World, the most henpecked of husbands into an ever scrawnier version of his former self; or for inclusion in a complete portfolio of photographs snapped by a myriad of enterprising Petulengros and Gypsy Lees all anxious to boast of his smiling patronage. One has a recurring mental image of a Blackpool peopled by the jesters who have paid heed to its professional call over the years. A sozzled Frank Randle appears to be propping up each Yates' Wine Lodge; a gruff Jimmy James and his two stooges are working a round-the-clock three-card monte on the sizzling prom; while a paunchy Dave Morris deals out deck chairs from behind his thick pebble-lenses in another confidence trick, this time with municipal backing. The high squeal of a sea-front tram signifies the irrepressible approach of Albert Modley at the wheel; a bustling Hylda Baker dispenses cockles, oysters and cans of tea; while hunched in a corner, exercising squatters' rights, are a gang of young rapscallions, Dodd, Tarbuck, More-cambe, Wise, waiting in the wings for the moment of takeover. But there is no mistaking the centre of attention, George Formby, at once the epitome of the working-class ideal of "one of us up there" and as such the undisputed King of Blackpool on his canvas throne, uku-lele doubling as orb and sceptre, knotted red polka-dot handkerchief for a crown, stemming the rain more successfully than Canute the tide. He was the one seaside entertainer not to need meteorological aid to ensure full houses. It is a makeshift dream, but then Blackpool, the place where madcap routine is replaced by an ever madder one, and where nobody is at all surprised at what anybody else might do, has nothing if not a dreamlike quality.

In direct contrast with numbers like "Swimmin' with the Wim-min'" and "Sitting on the Top of Blackpool Tower", there was one song which took Formby back to far more basic roots. "In a Little Wigan Garden" shifts one's attention to the bleaker environs of in-dustrial Lancashire life and reveals an affinity with a landscape distin-guished for its exhilarating ugliness, more in the comic-realist tradi-tion of Lowry than of McGill. Here he places himself securely in his father's shoes, displaying a humour that responds to the knuckle-grazing hardness of life with both vivid poignancy and a determined obduracy. Formby, forsaking "beautiful meadows and fields and your parks so grand", clings with loyalty to his postage-stamp of gravel which masquerades as a garden fighting a losing battle against the enveloping smoke and grime. This is an estate where crocuses croak with gasworks smog and he is forced to conduct his courtship amid scented breezes of a kind with which Casanova never had to con-tend:

In a little Wigan garden,
With me little Wigan knees,
Getting stung with bumblebees,
Between the cabbage and the peas;
'Neath the Wigan water lilies,
Where the drainpipe overflows,
There's my girl and me,
She'll sit on my knee,
And watch how the rhubarb grows.

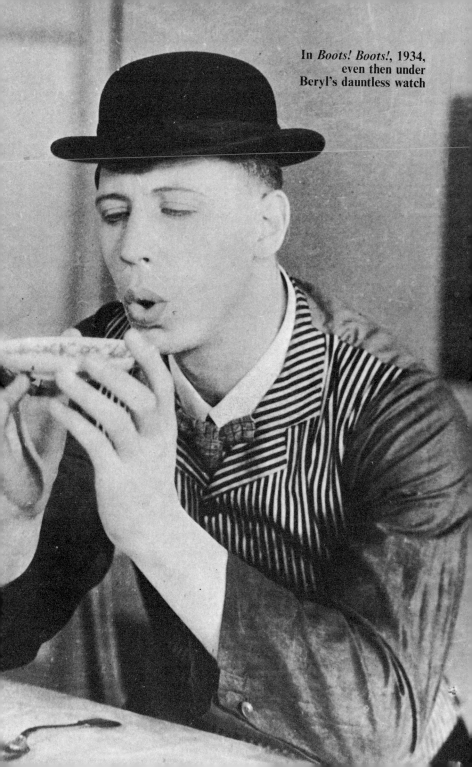

In *Boots! Boots!*, 1934,
even then under
Beryl's dauntless watch

The analogy with Lowry is not strained. Photographs of Formby's father with his huge feet and that comparatively spindly body, hunched at the shoulders, suggest that he could have walked out of a Lowry landscape. The grim gaiety that peeps through the bleakness of the artist's work also characterises another prominent Formby number. However much "Down the Old Coal Hole" may have concerned itself with the sexual shenanigans of George the miner at pit head, it never failed to convey the foul discomfort of a life belowground, the voice that sang it to suggest at that point lungs ravaged by pneumoconiosis:

> Give me my shovel and my pick, Nellie ...
> I'm going down the Hole to get the coal;
> With my meat and gravy canned,
> My little bundle in my hand,
> I'm going down the old coal hole.

Like all great artists Formby could endow commonplace detail, as displayed in that mundane lyric, with a richness and wonder that bedazzled even those in his audience who were hardened to it as an inescapable facet of everyday life.

Wherever he performed there were, of course, three songs without singing which he was never allowed to leave the stage: "Chinese Laundry Blues", "When I'm Cleaning Windows" and "Leaning on a Lamppost". Of these, "Chinese Laundry Blues" was the earliest, featured in his *Boots! Boots!* film of 1934, although without George singing it, merely as the accompaniment to Beryl's clog-dancing routine. That it became his signature tune might appear strange to those who find it hard to reconcile its Oriental motif with a comedian from such a sturdy Lancashire background. Such a reaction, however, fails to acknowledge the thriving Chinese population of that county in the 'thirties, particularly in Liverpool's Chinatown where as J. B. Priestley remarked on his *English Journey* in 1934, "a boy could look pure Liverpool and prove to be three parts Chinese". Without a trace of condescension the song concerns itself with the misadventures of one such Lancastrian Oriental, Mr Wu, whose laundry has been on the decline since he transferred his attention to a Chinese girl. The result is a calamitous chain of scorched underwear, shrunken vests and best Sunday shirts that finish life with "perforated rudders":

Bananas and dream!

Oh Mr Wu,
What shall I do?
I'm feeling kind of Limehouse Chinese Laundry Blues.
This funny feeling
Keeps round me stealing;
Oh won't you throw your sweetheart over do?

Eventually, oblivious of Formby's plea, he marries her instead, an excuse to launch a second song, "The Wedding of Mr Wu", with the ukulelified, ting-a-ling-ling, Oriental chimes of the Laundry Blues substituted for the Wedding March and the church decked out with the washing off the backyard line:

They broke a piece of china, then the marriage vow was read;
She took him home and broke a lovely teaset on his head.

This was the first song in a seemingly never-ending line that represents a virtual Chinese soap opera, comprising amongst others, "I'm the Husband of the Wife of Mr Wu", "Mr Wu's an Air Raid Warden Now" and "Mr Wu was in the Air Force". Mr Wu even became linked with the motif of the second song of the big three when in 1940 "Mr Wu's a Window Cleaner Now" indicated that the laundry had obviously failed to survive the Depression years and the onslaught of war:

> He had his eyesight tested, a most important matter,
> Through a bathroom window a lady he peeps at her.
> His eyesight's getting better,
> But his nose is getting flatter,
> 'Cause Mr Wu's a window cleaner now.

By contrast, the original "When I'm Cleaning Windows", recorded in 1936, featured George himself as worker as distinct from spectator, even though the job in hand provided both mind and eye with the most tempting of opportunities for wandering back from the task in hand to the onlooker's role. All who listen to it are reduced, like George, to inadvertent Peeping Toms, the individual thrill of "What the Butler Saw" now transformed into mass entertainment:

> At eight o'clock a girl she wakes,
> At five past eight a bath she takes,
> At ten past eight my ladder breaks,
> When I'm cleaning windows.

Dipsomaniacs who drink their bath-water, Talkie Queens divested of all make-up, honeymooning couples from whom the phrase "parlour tricks" assumes a new dimension, all fall under his prurient gaze. As long as the glazier's art provides its own transparent licence for voyeurism, George, self-styled "nosey parker" that he is, keeps the better side of respectability.

And yet, although it had already been featured in the film *Keep Your Seats Please*, the song still offended the BBC in its strait-jacketed, Reithian infancy. When someone requested the record on the air, the frustrated announcer, taking note of the NTBB sticker on its label, ("Not To Be Broadcast"), offered the feeble excuse that "The windows are too dirty". Things changed when Beryl, on George's behalf, made it clear that the full uncut version was a particular favourite of the Royal Family, of Queen Mary in particular; they not only got the record restored to the airwaves but no less than an apology immediately prior to the nine o'clock news, peak listening moment of the evening.

Nothing, however, should obscure the fact that given the remarkable facility of the British language whereby any word can be forced into a temporary, more risqué meaning simply by its context, George's songs were remarkably near the knuckle for their day. All things may be pure to the pure, and yet, in spite of the quaint, almost saint-like innocence which he could switch on, very few people were that refined not to know what he really meant when he sang of his magical wand, his gas mask, Mr Wu's chopstick, Auntie Maggie's Remedy, his Grandad's flannelette nightshirt, and, of course, his little stick of Blackpool Rock. At times the titles of his songs read like chapter headings for a veritable "Phallus in Wonderland". And if one was unsure of what a title really implied, as with, say, "I Wonder Who's Under Her Balcony Now?", one had only to wait a few lines for all to fall into place:

Is he kissing her under the nose
Or underneath the archway
Where the Sweet William grows?

As innuendo piled upon innuendo, it was inevitable that even the ukulele would not be exempt from a place in his special secret language. The original version of "With my Little Ukulele in My Hand" was in fact withdrawn before release by Decca, who insisted on the substitution of less offensive lines. Still, however audacious any of the songs appeared, they always just steered clear of explicit sex. Formby had a cunning habit of building up to a rhyme that conceivably might cause offence, only to substitute, after the requisite prim pause, a word totally out of place in the rhyme scheme:

In society I will soon make my bow,
Dressed up tricky,
With a clean – shirt on,
Hitting the high spots now.

He would even change 'hell' for 'heck', 'belly' for 'ankle'. But such a technique can only provide a superficial reason for why he got away with what he did. Besides, individual words conspicuous by their absence were often far more innocent than what was implied by whole lines. Formby himself once confided to songwriter Eddie Latta: "You know, some of the songs are a bit near. But they'll take them from me in evening dress; they wouldn't take them if I wore baggy pants 37 and rednose." He also had that double-purpose expression whereby the mouth formed a smile of glowing innocence, while the eyes knowingly perused the audience like frantic searchlights in their conspiracy to find the one person able to appreciate the double meaning that split second before anyone else.

Strangely, what is perhaps Formby's most famous song is devoid of all innuendo and comic intention. His treatment of "Leaning on a Lamppost", however, represents the most perfect expression of his charm, at once dignified, touching and humane. He inherited the motif of the shy casual bystander waiting on the pavement from his father's "Standing at the Corner of the Street", a fact that may have coloured his subdued interpretation. The new song is unashamedly sentimental in the infatuation it depicts on his part for the girl who may or may not appear, but not in a tacky flypaper way:

> There's no other girl I could wait for,
> But this one I'd break any date for;
> I won't have to ask what she's late for;
> She wouldn't leave me flat, she's not a girl like that.
> Oh, she's absolutely wonderful, and marvellous, and beautiful,
> And anyone can understand why.
> I'm leaning on a lamppost at the corner of the street
> In case a certain little lady passes by.

Formby would sing it from the day he recorded it in 1937 until the end of his career, never outgrowing it, perhaps because in his twilight years it did more than any other song to conjure up for his most stalwart fans the image of the younger Formby of the 'thirties.

While it may shun a comedic effect, however, it still bears a significant relationship with the other songs. The one quality Formby exudes above all others as he sings it is devotion. One looks beyond the lyric, to the time when the hopeful lover will leave his lamppost to marry some "little lady" and to embark on many years of domesticity, either cosy or calamitous. For Formby's basic audience, however hazardous the years of marriage might prove, however soon the couple lose their good looks and sex appeal, the institution will remain inviolate, the bond inviolable. Within this context, the song when backed by Formby's yearningly romantic treatment stands for the moral background outlined by Orwell as essential to the success

of a stable society, the moral code which provides the necessary

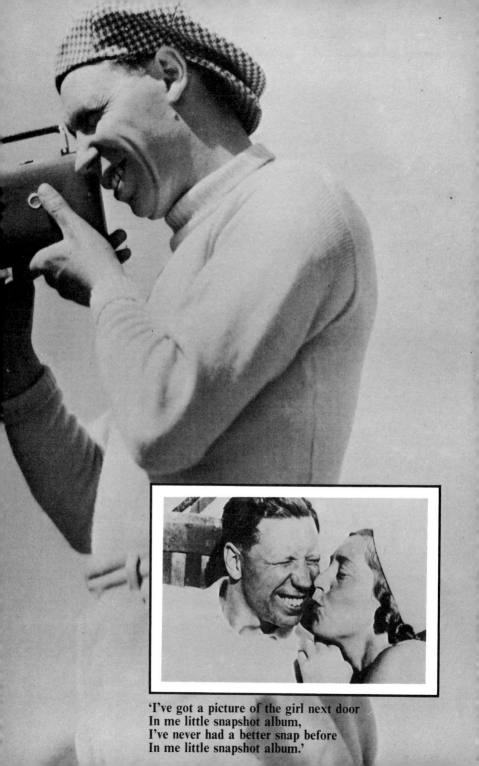

'I've got a picture of the girl next door
In me little snapshot album,
I've never had a better snap before
In me little snapshot album.'

springboard for all those jokes which adhere garishly to their postcard backing.

It is interesting to compare Formby with Max Miller, the only other British comedian to rival him at the theatre box office as a solo attraction in the 'thirties. Miller's strength, diamond hard and sharp, resided in the lengths to which he would overtly (or as overtly as possible) go in order to shun sexual respectability, to prove that this sort of status quo was not unshakeable; Formby, while taking a simple-minded naughty boy's delight in thumbing his nose at the restricting reality, never took the whole journey, curiously went part of the way towards setting up the "Aunt Sally" to be knocked down, at heart a roundhead to Miller's flashy sexual cavalier. These impressions informed their private lives, at least as presented by the media. Although he was happily married the press never seemed anxious to promote Miller as the doyen of domesticity; Formby's own marriage, while it would secretly deteriorate the more the business relationship it contained predominated, was until the end nothing if not public property, a prime model of connubial bliss. In the weeks before he

Max Miller, his only rival, with the Formbys on the Broads, 1952

died, Formby confessed: "The public built up a certain picture of us and I had no wish to spoil the illusion." One wonders if he ever thought back to the song he had jokingly recorded in happier domestic times in 1932, a song which openly advocated marital infidelity:

> Let's all go to Reno, that's a brand new notion;
> Let's all go to Reno, it's just across the ocean.
> Come with me and I'll give you the "hunch",
> How to get a new wife with ev'ry lunch;
> Divorces there are a tanner a bunch
> So let's all go to Reno.
> Eee – I've broke my marriage vows.... My Fair Lady!

It is the one song in the Formby repertoire that would have been improved had it been given the more piquant spice of Miller's own sexual attitude.

One can detect a similar moral undertow in Formby's sketches. He had an opening routine in which he would be constantly interrupted by people coming on from the wings in various stages of

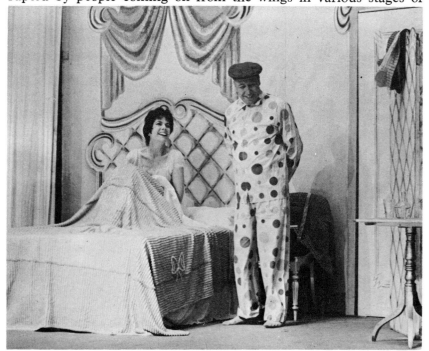

With Bettina Richman in the honeymoon sketch, Blackpool, 1960

undress anxious to claim – one of the hazards of everyone supposedly sharing the same dressing room – their missing garment, whether hat, coat, pants, from him. This proceeds until he is wearing nothing but vest, socks and a rather obvious pair of striped pants, at which point a girl appears sporting towel around her waist and a bra of the same striped material. Before she can ask to check the label George with a not too subtle double-take would explain, "Not bloody likely!", the cue for a blackout. Had Miller been playing the sketch he would immediately have headed off stage with the girl in the sexually most promising direction. Appropriately Formby's most famous sketch – part of the bread to the jam of his personality act in the George Formby Road Shows with which he and Beryl toured the leading provincial centres in the late 'twenties and early 'thirties prior to achieving film fame – was a contrived celebration of the marriage state, of the working-class attitude that regarded its consummation as the most exciting event in the average human being's life. It was little more than a repository for gags and business, all corn as high as the elephant's eye, evolving from the nervous attempts made by the groom – for once George in a cloth-cap, the zany complement to violently spotted pyjamas – to arrive in bed alongside his *négligé*-clad bride, long played by Beryl and already demure between the sheets as the curtain rises. Everything is done to stall for time: measuring the bed for size; checking under the bed; nervously taking a run at it to get in; falling short; shivering on the edge; checking its bounce only to hit hard against a plank, pretext for the typical creaking line: "Well, we won't get much sleep in there tonight, thank God – real seaside board"; the teasing innocence of the bride regarding her own role in the scenario; anything to add suspense to what they both know lies ahead. Not that they do come within clarion call of the sex act on stage. A telegram arrives from George's mother, conveying instructions *vis-à-vis* his investments in a Building Society, though of course misconstrued in the heat of the moment by a son sworn by his bride always to do what his mother says. "Do nothing till you hear from me", is the *coup de grâce* which neither can top in creating a spurious sense of adventure around the deed, in reinforcing the natural as the mysterious and unattainable.

While "Leaning on a Lamppost" would probably prove to be most people's favourite Formby number, it was not penned by any of his standard company of songwriters, a group headed by Harry

The favourite Formby song: one he didn't write

Gifford, Fred E. Cliffe (both responsible for "Windows"), Eddie Latta ("Remedy" and "Nightshirt") and Jack Cottrell ("Mr Wu"). "Lamppost" was the creation of Noel Gay, who around the time he was writing for Formby was also composing the equally infectious "Lambeth Walk" for Lupino Lane. Ironically it was the one occasion when Beryl for all her shrewdness was unable to cut her husband in on the creation of a song – namely, have his name appear as part-composer, as happened with most of them. The record in fact came after the film in which it first appeared, by which time Gay, assured of the success of his composition, held the trump card and insisted that if Formby wanted to issue it as a record, then the song, and its royalties, must be credited to no one but himself. It is doubtful if Formby ever did contribute creatively to his lyrics, although he always blithely insisted that he wrote all his own songs. As Eddie Latta stressed in a radio interview just before his death, "He could never write them, but by God he could pick 'em." To which, though, one

Back in the saddle, Epsom, 1938

should add that there are few Formby songs that would stand complete without his interpretation. If only by a process of osmosis the persona which *was* his creation must have influenced writers somehow.

While his composing talents may be questioned, however, there can be no doubt about his musical ability, as important to the success of the songs as either lyrics, voice or personality. He could not read music, nor could he tune his instrument. On stage he evaded the embarrassment of the latter by having a whole array of ukes on a settee, each one in a different key. Only when he spilt the beans on his last television show did audiences realise that this was not the gimmick they had always assumed. And yet that devastating high-speed right-hand syncopation, no doubt helped by the digital and wrist control developed as a jockey, has led to his being acclaimed by experts as the finest rhythm banjulele player this country has known, the creator – by a process of both trial and error and intuition – of the style that made him famous, and which he always featured minus lyric as his songs drew to a close, a sequence technically labelled "sequence of seven followed by stop, roll, bounce, and flicker". It is impossible to imagine either his act or his films without his shuffling background rhythms. He paraded his musical technique as insistently as if it were some egotistic symbol of authority or virility. For all his basic gormless innocence, he could always bring out his uke, like Shakespeare's clowns their "tabor and pipe", to win a modest self-respect, to insinuate gently that he wasn't quite the fool he might seem.

Formby's own attitude to the songs in his films was one of suspicion: "Even in my own films I always felt they came to a stop whenever I had to play the uke. When that was finished we could get on with t'fun." And yet the musical interludes were what the public wanted, his producers racking their brains constantly to devise ways of integrating them into haggard plots. The excuses were often as contrived as the expressions on the faces of the extras used for reaction cutaways during the number. In "Feather Your Nest", for example, he only gets to sing "Leaning on a Lamppost", the song that would more than any other become incontrovertibly *his*, after he has smashed the master disc of the song as recorded by another singer and, in a desperate attempt to save his job, broken into the recording studios to cut his own version. It was not so much a case of the songs holding up the plot as *vice versa*. It didn't matter that he should break into song for no other reason than that he just happened to find himself in a music shop, to spot someone in the crowd holding a uke. The film one would have most welcomed from Formby was never made, in spirit a carefree ukulele-tour of all the stepladders from which a nosey parker ever peered, all the lampposts against which a naive lover ever wistfully leaned. A. Crooks Ripley vividly described Formby in *Spectacle* as "Don Quixote with a guitar for mule; riding it reinfree, sack fashion, through the stage doors of Middlesbrough, South Shields, Hartlepools, via Ealing to Blackpool". Without realising it he was providing the scenario for a musical which, had Ealing been Hollywood, would have given birth to itself.

48 **Willie Waterbucket among the souvenirs**

The pure gold screen

Nothing, however, would prevent Formby remaining the greatest commercial success cinema-wise of all the top British comedy names who in the 'thirties lent their talents to the screen. If one excludes his appearance at ten years as the stable lad who outwits a gang of criminals in a pre-Dick Francis, pre-talkies, racing thriller *By the Shortest of Heads*, a gesture from a father, anxious that his son should have nothing to do with show business, to friend and producer Will Barker, his first film, *Boots! Boots!*, a crude "quota-quickie", was shot in 1934, in a one-room studio over a garage in London's Albany Street. The ramshackle conditions both he and Beryl, co-starring to cut costs, were prepared to endure – before shooting could commence it was necessary to ring a bell to stop the clatter of engines down below – and the salary of £100 a week for two weeks plus 10 per cent of the profits (compared with the £35,000 a picture he could command only a few years later), are indicative of his determination to break into the new medium. The budget for the entire film was only £3,000. George later admitted, "Ooh, it was a lousy picture. Ooh, it was so dark in places you had to strike matches to see it." However bad it may have been, the following year he was asked back to make a second, *Off the Dole*, at the same time that Basil Dean, overlord of Associated Talking Pictures at Ealing Studios, was searching desperately for another personality to match the appeal of Gracie Fields, George's spiritual sister, at the box office. The success of his first two films in the North led to an Ealing contract under which he would make eleven films between 1936 and 1941, before entering another contract worth £500,000 with Columbia, for whom he would make seven more between 1941 and 1946. Consistently throughout the war years he proved himself to be Britain's highest-paid entertainer, and for six consecutive years from 1938, on the evidence of the Motion Picture Herald Poll, the country's top cinema box-office attraction, a record still to be beaten. At the height of his popularity, his fan mail amounted to 90,000 letters in a single year, membership of the George Formby Fan Club numbering over

Wicked thoughts with Kay Walsh, *I See Ice,* **1938**

52 **The film of the catchphrase, 1941**

21,000. His popularity extended to almost every country of the world, including the USSR where, as a result of a showing for British sailors in a Murmansk cinema, *Let George Do It* ran for a year in Moscow with dubbed dialogue and the new title, with deference to the concert party in J. B. Priestley's *The Good Companions*, "Dinky Doo". In 1944 a Russian poll showed George himself to be the most popular figure in Russia after Stalin and for a while the balalaika must have felt a threat from the banjulele. The only obstacle to global acceptance appeared to be the USA, where his films commanded only second billing, if that, and, as Norman Wisdom would find out twenty years later in an almost carbon-copy situation, people were unable to come to terms with the obsessive grass-roots tradition of British comedy. And yet had he been given the opportunity to film in America, where the treatment of the music-hall comedian was never as paranoiacally scriptbound as it was here – witness the beginnings of American film comedy, beginnings never completely disowned, a simple attempt to capture on celluloid the magic of basically vaudeville performers like Chaplin, Keaton, Fields, Laurel, with little concession to cinematic technique – he might well have broken the barrier.

His film success is not difficult to understand. His characterisation of the good-natured, gormless fool always stumbling and miscalculating, not totally sure of the basic demarcations of time and place and rank in which nature has set him and reality is imprisoned, fitted with shoe-horn ease into formula plots which allowed him to rise triumphant after foiling the baddies through a combination of luck, high spirits, and that dose of guile that was as the donkey's kick in his overall doltish image. In short, he was the born survivor in a world swamped by bewilderment, bafflement and hostility. Where Formby becomes memorable, and Wisdom loses out, is that within this mêlée there is no room for tears, no open craving for sympathy. You so much *wanted* him to win the race or get the girl, that there was, in fact, little time to feel sorry for him along the particular obstacle course set down by that movie. When that obstacle course was not a comment upon service life (*It's in the Air*, *Let George Do It*, *Get Cracking*, *Bell Bottom George*), it guyed a recognisable trade (George as a bus conductor in *Keep Your Seats Please*, a jockey in *Come on, George*, a policeman in *Spare a Copper*, an artist in *Much Too Shy*), or current craze or obsession (the 'thirties preoccupation with Health and Beauty in *Keep Fit*, ice-skating in *I See Ice*, spies in *South American George*,

Spare a Copper, 1941

With Pat Kirkwood, *Come on George*, 1940

With Phyllis Calvert, *Let George Do It*, 1940

...'s In The Air, 1939

'Ooh Mother!'

national release in *George in Civvy Street*). Always, however, his view of the action tallied with the title of a later service farce, *Worm's Eye View*, made famous on stage by Ronald Shiner, a recruit from Formby's own basic film repertory company.

The films had no artistic pretensions, were all as simple and unsophisticated as tripe and trotters, but because rather than in spite of this managed to convey something of the natural exuberance that burst from Formby on a stage. The linchpin here was that batter-pudding face with the smile that, when you thought it had been stretched to its smiliest, could, through a subtle shift of the eyelids, be made to appear even more radiant still, together with the most mobile of pupils adding character like currants as they worked over-time darting from one side of the screen to the other when anger or enthusiasm was aroused. Aside from an ability to burn its image onto the retina of the screen, it was nothing if not an honest face, a quality which informs his entire *œuvre*, the work of a man who according to Basil Dean himself was a shrewd judge of his own capabilities and refused ever to step outside of them. Even if someone had gone to the lengths of building an open-air theatre on Wigan Pier, nothing would ever have moved George to play Hamlet.

Film making entailed two express bonuses for Formby, the prospect of additional feminine company and an opportunity to indulge that spirit of adventure already seen active in his songs. He didn't scare easily and once accepted a £5 bet from Northern impresario Jack Taylor to climb the outside – all 500 feet – of Blackpool Tower, a wager he would have carried out had not Ealing threatened to break his contract for risking the neck of its most valuable property. He had a passion for speed – is on record in 1939 as the first person to drive round Brooklands at 100 mph – and this trait was put to constructive use in his films, which always featured an erratic hair-raising chase towards their end, a chase with madcap fury rather than Keatonian subtlety as its keynote. It is doubtful if he enjoyed making any film more than *No Limit*, the first under his Ealing contract, because of the chance it offered him to prove himself a primeval Knievel of the 'thirties. He loved motorcycles way beyond the expensive cars he seemed to hoard, mere tokens of an extraneous life style, and in his attempts to win the TT Races did most of his own stunting, on an old AJS he had built himself and christened the "Shuttleworth Special". In *Come On, George*, a horse-racing drama with Formby

'Biceps, Muscle, and Brawn': with Guy Middleton, *Keep Fit*, 1938

as jockey, no stuntman is used at all, while the most exhilarating moments of *Spare a Copper* occur when the identity of his motorbike becomes blurred with that of a steed, George in person magically guiding it through, round and over the hazards of a point-to-point

'In a fifty mile race, I am the best, I ride five miles and skid the rest', *No Limit*, 1936

field. *Let George Do It* finds the stuntman again redundant as our hero swings from balcony to balcony on a rope of balloons before clinging precariously to a chandelier that in turn plummets to the floor. With the exception of Harry Langdon, no comedian so unathletic in appearance proved in fact to be so spry.

His reward at the end of every chase was, of course, the hand of the girl who, for all she may have seemed disappointed when his nerve did fail, had trusted in his simple faith all along, in spite of the competition he faced from inevitably smooth, smart-aleck rivals. He always had difficulty in dating the girl in the first place, but luckily was never at a loss for a song with which to cover up his embarrassment. Ironically, the words themselves often depicted George as a veritable Lothario in song:

> That night at 12 o'clock, just as the light she turned out,
> "Who's that in my room" she cried, and started to shout.
> I whispered, "Shut-up, I'm the ghost I told you about.
> Perhaps you'll believe it now."

Even one with an imaginative line in birth control:

> There's a baby born they say
> Every clock tick – that's O.K.
> I bought a sundial yesterday;
> They can't fool me.

The girls in his films were all as sexless as Walt Disney's Snow White, as hard to reconcile with the under-the-counter lustfulness of his lyrics as his own apple-for-the-teacher innocence. Pat Kirkwood, a rising soubrette in musical comedy and variety when she took time out to make *Come On, George* in 1939, remembers with anguish how her long tresses were shorn and she was forced into the dowdiest of dresses for the part of the policeman's daughter which "might have been the part of a sixty-year-old suffragette by the time I stepped before the cameras". It was some time after filming was completed before she discovered that it was on the instructions of Beryl that she had been "deglamourised", and a sexy, pre-Monroe gag whereby her skirt was blown up around her panties by a fairground wind-machine had been vetoed. It had long been common knowledge that after *No Limit* and *Keep Your Seats Please* (with Florence Desmond), and *Keep Fit* and *I See Ice* (with Kay Walsh), Beryl had ensured,

and would continue to do so, that he had a different female co-star in each film. Apart from Beryl in *Boots! Boots!* the only leading lady he got to kiss full on the lips was Googie Withers at the end of *Trouble Brewing*, when both are capsized in a brewery fermenting tank. Before shooting, director Anthony Kimmins had given the secret instruction "Make it a whopper!" to Miss Withers. Garry Marsh, the most prominent supporting actor in the Formby films, recalls how, when the deed was done, Beryl "hit the roof", as she did the night at the Palladium when Billy Cotton insisted it was all right for him actually for once to get between the sheets in the honeymoon sketch which, now late in their lives, he was playing with Audrey Jeans: "Sure, it's all right. I've had a word with Beryl."

It is hard to say which was more persistent, Formby's roving eye for a pretty girl, or Beryl's beady eye keeping dauntless watch on the set at every take. Certainly a reputation preceded Formby as, in Miss Kirkwood's phrase, "a frustrated Casanova" – or not frustrated, if one considers the public flaunting of his songs their own means of wish-fulfilment - but this was doubtless exaggerated in the light of his wife's maniacal jealousy, so intense that according to Irene Handl, who played with George in *Get Cracking*, "You only had to say 'good morning' and she thought you were asking him to bed." As long as Beryl played her oppressive role of Dragon Empress to his Mr Wu, it is not surprising that on the rare occasions when she broke her customary vigil, George should adopt an attitude of "now or never". Monja Danischewsky, the publicity director at Ealing at the beginning of the war, recalls how when Beryl opted out of the final afternoon's shooting of *Spare a Copper* in favour of a hair appointment, "having no doubt extracted from poor George a promise not to talk to any strange women or accept sweets from them", he leapt at the chance of a lifetime and propositioned his leading lady, Dorothy Hyson, on her way from the canteen. The dialogue that ensued was later reported to Danischewsky as follows:

'Hello, Love ...'
'Hello, George!'
'Well – it's the last day on the picture.'
'Yes, it is, isn't it?'
'Have you enjoyed it, then?'
'Very much, thank you, George.'

'Would you like to do another picture with me, then?'

'Of course I would, George. I'd love to.'

'I can put in a word for you, you know. They have to take notice of what I say.'

'Oh, *do*, George. That's very kind of you!'

'Beryl's gone to town.'

'Oh, has she?'

'So what about coming to my dressing-room for a bit of fun?'

Miss Hyson in amused embarrassment protested with all the tact she could muster: "I'm sorry, George, but I just don't do that sort of thing. I really don't." "Oh, well!" sighed the comedian, "I'll have a cup of tea instead", and with a shrug of resignation, he proceeded to the canteen. Albert Modley recalls an occasion when George took a fancy to a girl in the chorus at the Blackpool Opera House. He specially bought a pair of stockings – at a time when they were scarce – as a device to effect an introduction in the wings. He sneakingly looked for his opportunity and had no sooner pounced than he turned round and beheld the awesome Brünhilde figure of Beryl watching him. With that spur-of-the-moment guile that belied the gormlessness in his stage characterisation, he explained: "This girl has brought you a pair of stockings. Isn't it good of her?" "Thank you very much," smiled Beryl, taking custody of the contraband goods. When Garry Marsh suggested to an overworked George that the two men should take a night off on the town together, Beryl's reply was equally curt: "D'you know what would happen if he went out with you? He'd come home in the early hours of the morning, stinking drunk, with lipstick all over his chops. No, he's coming home with me, aren't you, George?" That was that!

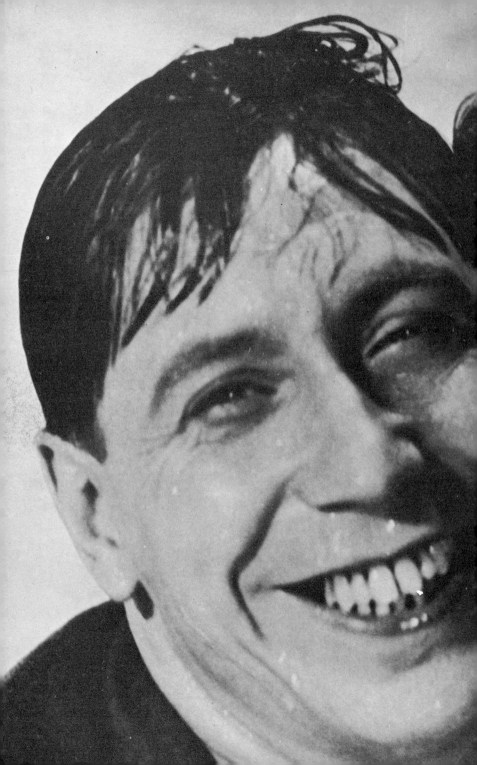

In the vat with
Googie Withers,
prior to *that* kiss,
Trouble Brewing, 1939

Married to the job

One advantage of Beryl's possessiveness was that his public image remained intact. And yet here one enters a vicious circle. It is precisely because the persona remains so concretely formed, the antithesis of a chameleon, that a fascination attaches itself to discovering what the man was really like beneath. Chevalier gave away part of the secret of star quality when he defined it as the ability to make people want to know about you. However, to find out about George, whether off stage he lived up or down to the role of the awestruck provincial the public paid to see, you had to penetrate the line of defence set up by Beryl. Danischewsky recalls that business with Formby was "rather like dealing with an interpreter". Because of this few people amongst those who worked with him felt they knew him. Reg Dixon, who took over the star spot from George during the run of *Zip Goes a Million*, was amazed how when he came off after the first-act finale of his own opening night, the rest of the cast parted like the Red Sea and froze at the side of the stage to give him right of immediate access to his dressing room. He couldn't understand why he got such treatment, until it was explained that Beryl had insisted on it from the beginning of the run for George to get to his dressing room without being waylaid. He also had most of his meals in his dressing room, cooked by Beryl on a portable stove. The same applied to filming. Pat Kirkwood doubts if she spoke more than ten words to him off camera. It is not surprising that few got to know him; got to know just how "gormless" – a word he encouraged – he really was.

If one pieces together the evidence from those who did get closest – however relatively so – to him, it suggests that he was shrewder than he appeared. Eddie Latta found him "a hard-headed Lancashire lad – there was nothing gormless about him. He went to the top. And he did it by his own decisions." Maybe the most crucial of those decisions was a conscious one to delegate to Beryl the role of go-between. Both Benson Dulay and John and Bettina Jackson, the two variety acts which worked most consistently with him on tour, agree that Beryl

Beryl keeping up appearances even on tour

was the frontwoman, the one who remonstrated with the MD when the band played too loud, haggled over contracts and billing with testy theatre managements, while George sat outside in the Rolls, sipping his favourite drink of tomato juice laced with an overdose of Worcester Sauce, and not shifting until the matter was settled in his favour. It is questionable whether anyone else's wife would have been allowed to interfere in the way Beryl did, had George not had some say in the situation. With this arrangement, admirably summed up by the slogan that persisted at Ealing, "Roll out the Beryl", he cunningly got what he wanted and at the same time appeared nothing if not the nice guy and dedicated performer, to whom a fit of temperament was as foreign as leaves in a Wigan street. In a newspaper interview Beryl herself once summed up the situation: 'George's only connection with business is writing autographs. I think a comedian shouldn't have business worries and George likes to feel carefree. He hasn't had a row with anyone in show business. I do all the battling. Everyone says George is a nice fellow but "she's a hot one". I don't mind what they say about me. I do mind what they say about George.' And so did George. A song again provides its own appropriate comment on the situation:

> Now I've a simple nature;
> Some folk think I'm dense.
> They think I'm slow,
> But I can show
> That I've got common sense.
> We come from monkeys, yes alas,
> Some say we've reached a lower class,
> But each time I look in the glass,
> They can't fool me.

One searches his life for evidence that he really lived up to these words, flashes of that wily independence which would corroborate the ruse. Maybe there was a flicker of a truer Formby in the aggressive little squirt he played in *Boots! Boots!*, a characterisation far removed from the one with which he sustained his popularity. His on-screen abrasiveness certainly corresponds with the approach he made afterwards to director Bert Tracy, also the chef in the film. According to Tracy, Formby complained afterwards that he would never make another film, that he was tired of being pushed around. Later when he did come to make *No Limit* with Florence Desmond, he was more than quarrelsome in expressing his distaste at her efforts to assert her co-star billing – Miss Desmond's contractual right – in the advertisements for the film that smothered their transport on location. There can be no question that he possessed a highly competitive streak, evident in his very decision to enter show business, to spite a plagiarist of his father's material; in the determination which took him to the lengths of writing his own script to secure a start in the movies; and as late as the Second World War in the satisfaction with which he could boast of his hat-trick in being the first entertainer to follow the invasion forces into Italy, Sicily and Normandy.

However tenacious he may have been, it is likely that Formby was quite incapable of playing a political game, a suggestion supported by the observation, however biased, of his later fiancée, Pat Howson, that "he was incapable of lying in personal relationships". But while Beryl would more and more assume responsibility for the dirty work that had to be done, there is no doubt, according to Bill Logan, the Carlisle businessman who became a close friend during their last five years, that "she enjoyed doing these rough tough jobs. She was the hatchet woman for George Formby." There was a relish in the way she flaunted her authority: "I just used to say all the time, if you want George, you've got to have me. And they always wanted George, so they *had* to put up with me!" In time, though, her self-importance became top-heavy, and fired by sexual jealousy she became George's taskmaster as well as servant, exerting a brutally intimidating hold upon him. Doggedly she would time his act with a stop-watch in the wings at each performance. Hughie Green remembers the scene she created if he overran a song by as little as six seconds. She restricted him to a stringent daily allowance of five shillings, as she took scrupulous care of the hard-won thousands, an impregnable nest egg from which, from the day in the mid-'thirties when they had amassed £50,000 in hard cash, she allowed George – no doubt as a safety valve whereby his attention was diverted from the girls – the luxury of two cars, a new Rolls Royce included, every year. And yet still when he gave Garry Marsh £1 to place on a horse at Northolt Racecourse he had to explain it away: "Ah've been saving oop." There is, though, nothing to indicate that he could not have tended his fortune as shrewdly as Beryl. Once Eddie Latta arranged for one of the Rolls Royces to be re-painted by a high-quality coachbuilder. George was

'Beryldene', one of many shrines to apparent domestic bliss

Bell Bottom George, relaxing through the fifties

more than pleased with the job. Within two days he had sold the car and made £500 profit. With income tax at 19s 6d in the pound, transactions on the side like this were as good as working.

In time their business relationship would make deep inroads on their marriage. One rumour, which no one close to them is keen to confirm, insists that Beryl had herself sterilised to prevent children interfering with the Rolls-Royce-smooth running of their mutual career. Within time, as more and more he came to resent the marionette's role he found himself playing attached to her strings, she would emasculate him, his life in Danischewsky's phrase eventually "that of a man permanently under house arrest". Beryl's dominance in the relationship becomes easier to understand when one recalls she gave up a performing career of her own to steer George on the road to stardom and ensure that he stayed at the top once he got there. Yet throughout she retained a vivacious attraction which could have made her a star in her own right had circumstances permitted. Doubtless the older she got, the more resentful she became of the lost opportunity. There was never a time when according to Mrs Nat Jackley she didn't "sparkle like Blackpool Illuminations: she mesmerised everything and everybody". She had a penchant for sequinned stockings, expensive furs, and birds-of-paradise hats. When she no longer appeared with George in his sketches, she continued out of sheer frustration to stake her claim to a share of the limelight. At the end of his act, she would always emerge with Queen Mary splendour to take the heartiest round of applause as if it were her own show as well as to confirm the image of married bliss. Years later Morecambe and Wise, with the buxom Janet Webb, would turn her effrontery into a gag, assigning it a special place in their own personal armoury of surefire comic motifs. One thing she refrained from was to burst out singing those meaningful lines from "Windows":

> In my profession I work hard,
> But I'll never stop.
> I'll climb this blinking ladder
> Till I get right to the top

It was a philosophy, however, that doubtless drove both of them.

As the business-in-marriage relationship rebounded on him at the expense of his home life, so Formby increasingly found his real home on stage. With significant irony magician Benson Dulay defined his

Hitting the high spots with Florence Desmond, *No Limit*, 1936

appeal before the footlights as that of a family man. Certainly his love of an audience and the great warm gusts of its appreciation betokened a simple need for affection, one of the reasons why he kept working into the 'fifties in spite of ill-health and one of the biggest personal fortunes ever gathered in British show business. The more home assumed the impersonal nature of the borrowed hardshell of the soft hermit crab, the warmer, more secure his performance became. Pat Howson once confided to Alan Randall: "That's probably why he was so great: he was kept down so much. When he got on stage it all came out." Once he was in the spotlight he could have taken a stick to the serried rows of stalls before him without losing an atom of approval, the rapport between him and them as contained and controllable as the flow of sand in an hourglass. Perhaps this is the most important clue in the identification of the "real" George Formby. One quotes Jean-Louis Barrault in a recent radio interview: "In real life do we truly know who we are? One may go on the stage to lose oneself; but, contrary to what one imagined, one may also be finding oneself." The ease with which people who never met him felt that they knew him, coupled with the difficulty of those who did meet him in getting to know him, suggest the real George Formby was the one the public saw most often. If this is so, one's picture of the comedian is incomplete without fuller reference to the audience who were as flesh to his bones.

A comic at war

Any entertainer only ever succeeds because he corresponds to a specific moment in time; to understand the loyalty of the Formby public one has to go back to the 'thirties, a decade now epitomised far more vividly by the voice once likened to a "fire bellow masquerading in the top register of a mouth organ", than by the school of revolutionary poets, whose despair is now fashionably held to be so representative, when only a small percentage of the population had heard of them. Once his film and recording careers had hit their stride, there can hardly have been a single moment of any day from 1935 until the end of the war when the voice of George Formby was not to be heard somewhere in England. Like a warm blade in dripping it cut clean through the general gloom of dole-queue fear, economic recession and Nazi alarm, even when, as in *I Could Make a Good Living at That*, the film doffed its cap at the root of the anxiety itself:

> I just can't remember the last time I worked;
> I could blush with repentance and shame.
> When I think of the years that I've spent on the dole,
> Well, I can't bear the sound of my name.

Everything about him spelt out a grim determination "to grin and bear it", as workers at their lathes and looms throughout the country quickened to the Formby beat, and hope was strummed out of murky air.

By birthright Formby's Northern roots more than qualified him for the role – there hardship grated hardest. But Formby was more than a Lancashire comic. He might have a fixation about inserting "black puddings and tripe and trotters" for no reason whatsoever midway through a song as irrelevant culinarily as "Count Your Blessings and Smile"; for all he would play the fool his whole attitude might be as down to earth as that placarded Northern philosophy: "Don't Talk Tripe, Eat It"; but his example was to the whole of Britain. Helped by his easy transition into the mechanised media available to him, he became the first national comic this country ever

had, and that in a pre-television age when a Southern genius like Max
Miller, a Northern one like Frank Randle, fought shy of appearing
North and South of Nottingham respectively. Where a Northern
comedian had made inroads on London taste in the past, as George
Formby Senior had done briefly, it had been by way of debunking
his roots. His son didn't; he cheekily celebrated them.

So vividly did he catch the mood of the country that when war
came he went into overtime. When he was not filming, he was proving
himself ENSA's most active performer, strumming his way with
Beryl through virtually every theatre of war, entertaining an estimated
three million troops, often in slit trenches within as little as eighty
yards of the front line. Songs like, "He Does Look a Swank Does
Frank on his Tank", "Guarding the Home of the Home Guard",
"Cookhouse Serenade" and "Imagine Me in the Maginot Line":

> Hitler can't kid us a lot;
> His "secret weapon's" tommy rot;
> You ought to see the one the Sergeant's got
> Down on the Maginot Line.

'Midst shot and shell, it's worse than, well, in fact it's worse than that!' Normandy, 194[4]

With Ben Lyon, Jack Warner, and Bebe Daniels, campaigning for the Tank Fund, Leicester Square, 1941

more than lifted morale and deflated tension all the way from battle front to munitions factory bench; they also gave to his record output the shot in the arm it would have needed before long to prevent it becoming stale. Research by Mass-Observation, the social survey organisation founded by sociologists Tom Harrison and Charles Madge, confirms what one had always guessed, that Formby was the greatest single morale booster during the hostilities, ahead of the usually accepted tie between Churchill and *Itma*. The songs were so accessible, so easy to carry in the head, that far away from wireless, gramophone or the performer himself, he became the easiest of all contemporary British entertainers to emulate, his chirpy spirit the easiest to evoke. Formby's importance was officially recognised when in January 1944 he was invited to step into the shoes of Ed Murrow and J. B. Priestley by broadcasting one of the Sunday evening Postscripts on his return from the Middle East. Dismissing his actual performances as unimportant, he stressed how it was *after* the performance that the show used really to start: "They wanted to talk to somebody from home. We used to sit around with mugs of tea, always tea, like a lot of old women gaffing, always about home – what was the beer like, was it getting stronger, how often does it rain, how is the food and cigarettes, and are the people being looked after. They were worrying quite a lot about you folks at home, but we soon put them right about that, Beryl and I; we told them that after $4\frac{1}{2}$ years at war Britain was still the best country to live in." The emphasis with which time and again on English soil he would stress of the troops: "They're better off over there than you are over here", belied the daunting conditions in which he himself was often forced to work. Basil Dean, by now overlord of ENSA, remembers a typical situation in Normandy: "Everywhere the stink of long-neglected dirt and the still fouler sweetness of death ... Standing with his back to a tree or a wall of sandbags, with the men squatting on the ground in front of him, he sang song after song, screwing up his face into comical expressions of fright whenever shells exploded in the near distance, and making little cracks when the firing drowned the point lines in his songs."

It would be facile to dismiss Formby's efforts as unthinking submission to a propaganda machine which he had to acknowledge for professional survival. Throughout the war he was noted for nothing if not his outspokenness. He protested violently at the way in which the best seats at concerts in more controlled surroundings were monopolised by officers and their wives; his request on one occasion for a telescope so that he could see the troops developed into a major row with the top brass. Officers' wives, however, were remarkably sparse at all subsequent concerts. He unwisely lashed out at other performers more conspicuous by their absence from the front lines, incurring the wrath of the Variety Artists' Federation with his outburst. A much-reported broadcast by Dean over All India Radio deprecating the special privileges demanded by other artists who "seem to have expected the order of battle should be altered to suit their convenience" brought the immediate response of a letter in protest to *The Times* signed jointly by Formby and Georgie Wood, though no doubt part-penned by Beryl, even though, as Dean has since insisted, "there were no stars in the ENSA firmament to whom my remarks applied with less reason".

It is difficult not to surmise from his apparent insatiability for 81 action that Formby, a man who, as one has already seen, liked to live dangerously, was consequently, as historian Andrew Hardman has said of Churchill, "a man who enjoyed war, and perhaps his contribution lay in communicating that enjoyment, in convincing other people that they too could enjoy war". It would account for the outspokenness and independence of spirit Formby showed in the war years. It would also ironically inform his rejection by the British film and recording industries and temporary eclipse in popularity once hostilities had drawn to a close. The man with the ukulele as much as the man with the big cigar had contributed to that sense of great common purpose which had pulled the nation through its conflict; the purpose now fulfilled, hope pointed forward and in so doing entailed the summary rejection of many of the elements that had led towards it. As Attlee and a socialist government ousted Churchill as PM, so James Mason took over from Formby as the country's top box-office attraction, himself ushering in a wave of so-called social cinema that rejected laughter for supposedly more worthwhile, though in retrospect phoney and depressing, ends. *Itma* survived because it had always remained on the more fanciful edges of the conflict; on the other hand Formby throughout was nothing if not the cocker spaniel to Churchill's bulldog, by contrast divested of all pomp and arrogance. At the heart of the action, he was the true representative of the working classes which, comprising most of the armed forces and heavy industry labour, were committed to fighting the enemy regardless. It is reassuring then that 1951, the year of Churchill's return to No. 10, should mark the return to Formby, now boasting a modest OBE for his wartime work, to the big time with the stage musical *Zip Goes a Million*.

Too much, too late

In the interim Formby shrewdly went out of his way to consolidate his reputation overseas with tours of Australia, New Zealand, Canada, South Africa and Scandinavia. Justifiably billed as "Britain's foremost comedian of stage and screen", in so far as none of his contemporaries could match his world-wide renown, he seldom failed to break house records, a fact that made his comment "Danny Kaye and Frank Sinatra come over here and take our dollars, so I ought to go back to Canada and bring back some more" even more appealing to the Treasury. In 1950 he was offered first a thirty-day tour of the USA and then a single Carnegie Hall concert for a "you name it, we'll pay it" fee not less than £15,000, but, unsure of a country where his films were little known – patriotism prevented him accepting an offer to film there during the war – he fought shy of the live American audience until the very end of his life when, no doubt trying to recapture the challenge of youth, he looked upon the prospect of playing Las Vegas as a horizon at last within reach. He never made it, but we do have some indication of how he might have fared. In 1971, Alan Randall, the most uncannily accurate of all Formby impersonators, played on a Las Vegas charity bill that included Jack Benny, Perry Como, Robert Goulet and Bob Newhart. Randall received a standing ovation and brought all the arguments about the barriers to understanding built into the so-called insularity of British humour tumbling down amid the applause.

It could be argued that with his success in Emile Littler's *Zip Goes a Million* at the Palace Theatre in October 1951, Formby was breaking down a barrier even more impregnable than the American one. It is the main cliché of his film career that for all his international success the films never found a place in the West End, where when they were shown you could, according to Sir Michael Balcon, "have shot a cannon-ball through the theatre without hurting anyone". Yet they would break records at cinemas as cavernous as the Dominion in Tottenham Court Road, like the 'live' Palladium and Holborn Empire, only two steps the other side of the arbitrary West End fringe. 83

Above and opposite: Rehearsals for *Zip Goes a Million*, 1951. Below: Beryl vies with the Duchess of Gloucester at a gala performance of the same show

PALACE MANCHESTER TEL. CENTRAL 01

WEEKS COMMENCING TUESDAY 18th

AT 7.0 MATINEES WEDNESDAY & SA

GEORGE FO

EMILE LITTL IN

"ZIP

GOES

MILI

VISITING MANCHESTER

THE PALACE THEATR

ONE 1

ONE 1

Idle Jack, the John Willie of panto, the Palace Theatre, 1956

Consequently, Formby had a complex about so-called West End so-phistication: "Fancy me and my ukulele on the stage where Ivor Novello knelt before the altar with a rose in his hand!" The show, however, was an astute blend of provincial knockabout and musical comedy, transatlantic style. Another lease of life for *Brewster's Mil-lions*, long cherished by Beryl as a possible vehicle for her husband, it featured George as Lancashire lad Percy Piggott, committed to spending, or rather squandering, but not giving, a million dollars in four months if he wishes to inherit a further seven millions, an exhilarating thought in post-war austerity Britain. It was a case of "Take seven letters – no, make it telegrams – they're more expensive!" The action took place predominantly in Texas and New York, but it was not difficult for the writers to include a cruise to a certain Raratonga Island, archetypal environment for a ukulele solo. It was Formby's show, a critical and popular success, crisply described by one critic as having the elegance of a Bond Street box with an Eccles cake inside and completely dispelling any doubts the comedian may himself have had that he couldn't, strictly speaking, follow in the footsteps of Novello and Buchanan – even if it was on his own shuffling flat-footed terms.

Sadly, he was not to sustain the success for long. After six months he suffered a severe heart attack which forced him to leave the show and threatened to end his career. Ironically, his own part was taken over by comedian Reg Dixon, famous for a catchphrase in direct descent from the tradition of Formby Senior, "Ooh, I'm not well. I'm proper poorly." Formby never fully recovered from his coronary condition, but kept going gamely, himself evoking the other side to his father's coin, as each appearance on stage became that much more of an effort. Within eighteen months he was back at the Palladium for a ten-week season in the revue *Fun and the Fair*, reviving with Audrey Jeans the honeymoon sketch at the top of a galaxy cast which included Billy Cotton and his Band, Terry-Thomas and the Deep River Boys. In 1956 he returned to the Palace Theatre to play Idle Jack in *Dick Whittington*. Then followed a comparative lull until summer seasons in Great Yarmouth in 1959 and Blackpool a year later, a lull notable only for the occasional provincial foray into farce: "Each year I find it harder to stay at the top and I didn't want to keep on playing the uke till I fade out." But still his variety self predominated. At a point in the action when he had the stage to himself, he would find a banjulele in its case, pick it up and with the sense of complicity of all great comedians turn to the audience: "Shall I?" The audience never left him in any doubt that the answer was 'Yes'. And he always hastily obliged before the next character made his entrance.

That he worked harder towards the end was no doubt to take his mind off the secret he kept from Beryl for three years, that she was dying from pernicious anaemia, later worsened by cancer. When she did die, on Christmas Day 1960, his heart gave way under the strain and he had to vacate the role of Mr Wu in his Bristol pantomime,

'Will you still need me, will you still feed me, when I'm 64?', March 1960

Aladdin. Less than two months later he announced his plans to marry a thirty-six-year-old schoolteacher, Pat Howson, whom he had known since she was nine. As George presented his fiancée with a diamond-studded ukulele brooch, his public, like his closest friends, were momentarily stunned into shock, forgetting the maxim that maybe the greatest compliment a husband can pay his dead wife is to re-marry as soon as possible.

As a result of the engagement his private life attained an even greater mystique than it had achieved before. As George begged his friends not to begrudge him the happiness he had at last found, so it all came spilling out, how the last fifteen years of happy marriage had been a mere façade, his Roman Catholicism clashing both with Beryl's atheism and with the thought of divorce to facilitate marriage to the future fiancée whom he had loved, without her knowing it, since 1954. "The public", he confessed to Michael Walsh in the *Daily Express*, "built up a certain picture of us and we had no wish to spoil the illusion", an illusion more difficult to sustain by reason of Beryl's excessive drinking, her one release from pain, by George's frustration in being unable to keep liquor from her, and by the rows between them that in later years thundered around through dressing room doors and thin back-stage walls culminating, that last summer season,

A birthday toast to his bride-to-be, February 1961

in Beryl being barred from the theatre.

Nine days before her death he appeared in a television "Solo Performance", the culmination of his entire career. Plumper and greyer, he proved that his rapport with an audience, whether at home or in studio, was still as taut and unslippable as a hawser, as he sang his famous songs and, in what was virtually a one-man "face to face", chatted his way through a lifetime's secrets. Without a trace of self-pity he revealed his musical limitations, his semi-illiteracy, and the part Beryl had played in his success. But the words, "I'll always be grateful to Beryl for doing all the business for me", were only half of the story. He went on to express his regret at not having a family, a regret underlined by his advice to the goldfish during his version of "Swim Little Fish", advice that of a frustrated parent as much as an engaging entertainer. At another moment tears welled to his eyes as he listened to a record of the father he wished he had known better. As Beryl watched from her hospital bed, his terrier Willie Waterbucket, guarding George's lucky charm, his father's last pair of stage shoes, listened from the dressing room. There were, in fact, three mascots in his life, but each was in its way ephemeral: the boots to represent the father he never knew; the dog in lieu of the child he never had; the wife who became an emotional cipher. He had

Solo Performance, **his last television show, December 1960**

everything, yet nothing, and before he could make amends, it was too late.

The excitement of his engagement proved too much and the coronary condition which he and Beryl had laughingly dismissed as Mr C.T. for so long – with a tragi-comic disregard for ill-health inherited from his father – took his life only ten days later on 6th March 1961. Mr C.T. was not to be laughed at. The outcome of his life was the total contradiction of the catchphrase with which he had always opened his act: "It's turned out nice again, hasn't it?"

More than funny

Formby once posed the question to journalist Alan Kennaugh, "If I'm not there in the limelight, do you know if people will remember me?" He need not have worried. Almost fifteen years after his death people still instantly pin the performer to the tune when his records are played. And while his songs are still anchored in the 'thirties and 'forties it is encouraging that the Beatles, fellow sons of Lancashire as well as the inventors of pop music as it is known today, paid more than a fleeting genuflection to Formby in their own heyday. The selectivity in the use of commonplace detail shared by both song canons goes without saying. More specifically, though, "When I'm Sixty-four" could, were its imagery not so knowing, have been written for Formby, a tribute to that cosy domesticity which informed his act from an age when marriage counts for less. George could well have imparted a second layer of meaning to lines like, "I could be handy mending a fuse, when your lights have gone", beyond the scope of McCartney himself. Listen carefully, though, to the Sergeant Pepper LP and you can almost hear Paul – in conscious homage? – essay a muted "he-he" at more than one point. Meanwhile records, in garish pop art sleeves that would have appealed to him, and sheet music of the original still sell, like hot cakes, barm cakes of course. Even in spite of the family wrangles which persisted over his will almost until Pat Howson, the main beneficiary of the £135,000 fortune, herself died in 1971, perhaps it really has "turned out nice again". It is certainly no exaggeration to speak of a Formby cult, of which the flourishing George Formby Society and Alan Randall's own success are only fringe manifestations.

The question that has to be asked of Formby, existing as he does beyond the period of which he was an appropriate symbol, is to what extent he would succeed today in an age of comparative permissiveness. Comedians like Benny Hill have proved, however, that lines like the following, based on the assumption that if someone shouts "knickers" the world will collapse in a heap, are still more than viable:

Now Mr Wu – he's got a naughty eye that flickers!
You ought to see it wobble when he's ironing ladies' – (prim
pause here) – blouses!

No doubt the laughter depends on context and anticipation, the word
trap of the lyric, as much as upon the breaking down of any taboos.
Otherwise, it is all a question of balance. It is an illusion that the fron-
tiers of what can be got away with have merely advanced. As they
have done so, new taboos have crept up in the rear. So while Formby
would have changed his act, he would not necessarily have broadened
it. Hill may now make jokes about homosexuals and drugs which
Formby would never have attempted; yet his own songs contain supposedly comic references to "loony asylums", physical deformity and
death, which would today be anathema to any comic as cheekily mild
and popular as Formby was then. Unlike Miller, Hancock, Dodd,
Formby never qualified as the funniest comedian in England at any
one time. He should not be assessed, however, on the volume of
laughter he raised. He came, partly through familiarity, partly
through the loyalty of his public, to transcend comedy. Like Lauder
before him and Bygraves since, he just *was*, all strolling troubadours
at heart with a string of easy to remember tunes and lyrics and an
ability to make you smile and feel happy without cracking an actual
joke; all men who could and can tell you how immensely popular they
are, how much they've made, and still remain a surprising humility.

92 **Towards the end of his life,** *still* **cleaning windows**

Strumming on a cloud

No two people's most vivid off-stage memory of the Ukulele Man will be quite the same. Some will remember a legendary meanness, the accepted corollary of twelve years struggling to get to the top of the bill and their attendant insecurity. Balcon recalls Formby's boast that he breakfasted in the Ealing canteen rather than at the Grosvenor House in Park Lane, a favourite London base, because the food was so much cheaper. Alan Randall recalls how each request at his dressing-room door for an autograph prompted the query from Beryl through the mere crevice of light she allowed into the room, "D'you want a picture?" The door would shut for the signing, to be reopened ajar with the sting, "That will be 2s 6d." His valet for twenty-nine years, Harry Scott, cannot recall seeing Formby, a heavy smoker himself, ever offering anyone a cigarette. The time he *was* seen to buy someone a drink at Ealing produced a reaction from onlookers comparable in Basil Dean's estimation with the one in the famous Bateman drawing of the guardsman who dropped his musket on parade. Others, like Reg Dixon, emphasise a less material generosity. Five months after his heart attack in 1952, George returned to the Palace Theatre to watch the man who had stepped into his enviable shoes. Afterwards he went backstage and carefully indoctrinated the younger comedian into all the gags and bits of business which, while not in the book, he had managed to sneak in, the legacy of a lifetime's experience. That way Dixon gained about six big belly laughs.

Another contemporary with a lot of time for Formby was Tommy Trinder. He remembers visiting his house, "Beryldene", at Poulton-le-Fylde. The first thing he noticed was the flamboyant wall panelling in the hall, made even more conspicuous by the initials G.F. carved upon it. "Is that George the Fourth?" queried Trinder. "Eee, no," grinned a bashful George, "it's George Formby." Tommy was then shown into his Chinese room, decorated as a would-be shrine to Mr Wu. On the wall was a scramble of Chinese characters. "What's that?" asked Trinder. "Eee, that's Chinese." "What does it mean?"

"That means George and Beryl." By this time Formby was becoming increasingly wary of his sharp, ad-libbing friend. "Really? who did it?" pumped Trinder. "Oh, local builder." "Get away," exclaimed Tommy, "he's caught you. That's not Chinese, it's Hebrew." Formby was adamant, "No." Nothing more was said on the subject. Three years or so passed before Trinder visited them again, this time on their cabin cruiser, "Lady Beryl", on the Norfolk Broads. When their conversation had come to a natural pause, Formby took the plunge: "Tommy, was that really Hebrew or was it Chinese?" He might have been gullible enough to trust the builder in the first instance, but he was shrewd and proud enough for the matter to prey on his mind all that time.

The one quality most alien to him was sophistication. When he put it on, as during one abortive attempt to play on the panel of *What's My Line*, with Beryl signalling the questions which he was supposed to ask from out of camera range, it stuck out like charity in Scrooge. On his return from a tour of Australia he explained to the Nat Jackleys, about to embark on a tour there themselves, why he hadn't enjoyed the continent. They almost collapsed when under their pressure he gave the reason why: "There's no bloody culture!" And he was serious about it too. The sentence became a domestic catchphrase for the Jackleys throughout their trip. The incongruity with which the remark dropped from his lips only stressed the simple tastes of a man whose own cultural level seldom transcended Flash Gordon, Superman and similar movie serials; a man who off-stage nursed no sartorial aspirations beyond an endless craving for parti-coloured pullovers, bought by the dozen; a man who for all his expensive cars loved most to tinker with his watches and motorbikes. As he described himself, "I'm the best in the world at doing nowt; a real champion at messing about."

One need look no further than his hit number from *Zip Goes a Million*, "Ordinary People", a song to rival "Leaning on a Lamppost" in its honesty and unfrivolous charm, for a summary of both his philosophy and art. Here Formby skirts miles clear of the irksome condescension that characterised the celebration of such folk in the Wilfred Pickles era, then at its height. His voice conveys the same humble dignity that underlined his assertion on that last television show: "We don't become stars. You people make us stars. We couldn't be anything without you. And any of our present stars today,

if they ever believe anything different, they're crazy." He meant it. And he deserved his success. From its start audiences had responded to each subsequent appearance he made on stage as an appeal for them all to recognise their common clay. In the words of another song he was:

> ... not stuck-up or proud,
> I'm just one of the crowd;
> A good turn I'll do when I can.

As for the Rolls Royces and the visits to Windsor Castle to entertain the King, well, they acted vicariously on behalf of his public, with George their representative, as near as they came to the experience themselves.

The writer Arthur Koestler justified his choice of England as a home with a quote from Orwell: "These crowds, 'with their knobby mild faces, their bad teeth and gentle manners, this nation of flower-lovers and stamp-collectors, pigeon-fanciers, amateur carpenters, coupon-snippers, darts-players and crossword-puzzle fans lived, in its muddled ways, closer to the text of the invisible writing than any other'." If so, then George Formby brought out that secret writing more vividly than any other British entertainer. Perhaps this is what actress Thora Hird was trying to express when in a recent radio tribute to him she said of his arrival in the after-life, "I reckon God probably said to him, 'I'm not gonna give you a harp, George. I'll just give you a ukulele.'" Only when a person dies do we learn the exact truth about our feelings towards him. No longer will people pretend to care if they are indifferent. It is Formby's greatest achievement that so many still do care, and their own consolation that, however simple his exterior, he was always knowing enough to accept that basic truth, shrewd enough to enjoy the success they brought him. I feel there are no more apt lines with which to close than five short ones by Roger McGough entitled, "Clown's Love Poem". You have to imagine George speaking to Beryl:

> Away from the laughter
> the lights
> the applause
> I'm nobody's fool
> only yours.

The "could-have-been" words of an extraordinary ordinary man.